ER COMMON

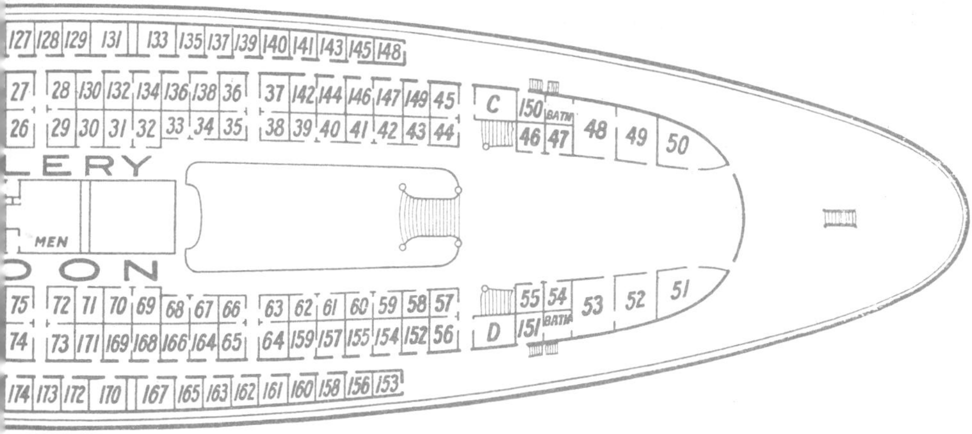
127 128 129 131 133 135 137 139 140 141 143 145 148
27 28 130 132 134 136 138 36 37 142 144 146 147 149 45 C 150 BATH 48 49 50
26 29 30 31 32 33 34 35 38 39 40 41 42 43 44 46 47
LERY
MEN
OON
75 72 71 70 69 68 67 66 63 62 61 60 59 58 57 55 54 53 52 51
74 73 171 169 168 166 164 65 64 159 157 155 154 152 56 D 151 BATH
174 173 172 170 167 165 163 162 161 160 158 156 153

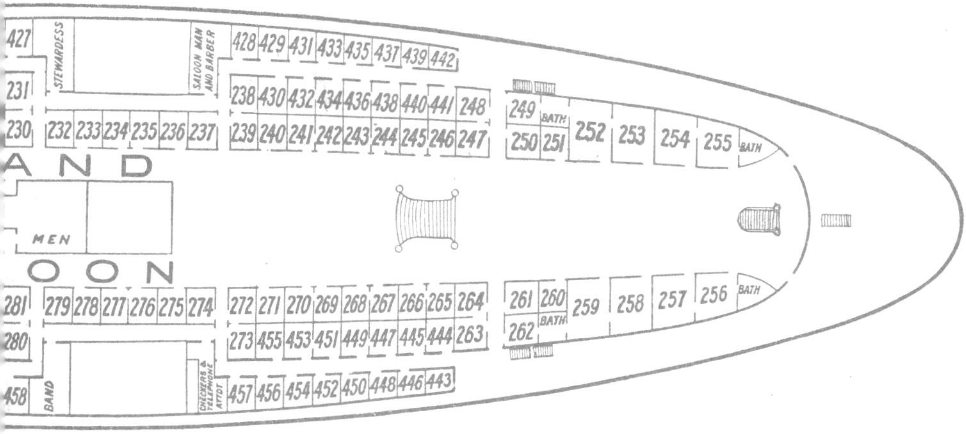
427 STEWARDESS SALOON MAN AND BARBER 428 429 431 433 435 437 439 442
231 238 430 432 434 436 438 440 441 248 249 BATH 252 253 254 255 BATH
230 232 233 234 235 236 237 239 240 241 242 243 244 245 246 247 250 251
AND
MEN
OON
281 279 278 277 276 275 274 272 271 270 269 268 267 266 265 264 261 260 259 258 257 256 BATH
280 273 455 453 451 449 447 445 444 263 262 BATH
458 BAND CHECKERS & TELEPHONE ATT'DT 457 456 454 452 450 448 446 443

COMMONWEALTH

Giantess of the Sound

Books by
ROGER WILLIAMS McADAM

THE OLD FALL RIVER LINE
New enlarged edition 1955

PRISCILLA OF FALL RIVER

SALTS OF THE SOUND
New enlarged edition 1957

COMMONWEALTH
GIANTESS OF THE SOUND

COMMONWEALTH

Giantess of the Sound

ROGER WILLIAMS McADAM

STEPHEN DAYE PRESS
New York

Printed in the United States of America

Library of Congress Catalog No. 59-11668

To my dear friends,

ANN and CHARLIE CLARK,

sharers in many a

memorable

COMMONWEALTH

voyage

Foreword

Several of the author's notable voyages on the COMMONWEALTH, of the beloved Fall River Line, are cited in the text. But there is one other, made in boyhood, which may have profoundly influenced the writing of this book.

On a breezy, calm, starry night some four decades ago, three persons stood immediately below the COMMONWEALTH's darkened pilothouse. One was a lad (the author), traveling alone to Newport. Standing close by was a couple. The conversation, in which the boy was not a participant, is as vivid as if it had been heard last night. The gentleman knew the pilot on watch (Albert T. Rowland), for he called him by name and engaged him in friendly discussion. Turning to his feminine companion the man voiced a tribute which found a permanent place in a boyish heart. "Millie, this COMMONWEALTH is *the greatest boat in the world.*" The *greatest*—no limiting adjective! In the *world* —no restriction of territory!

Sentimentally, as the years moved on, the author regarded Fall River's noble PRISCILLA as "queen of all American steamboats"; yet his loyalty was constantly challenged by those ringing words, "COMMONWEALTH is the greatest boat in the world." Having written the full story of PRISCILLA's glorious career, it is now the author's privilege to do the same for PRISCILLA's companion of twenty-nine summers, COMMONWEALTH, giantess of the Sound.

One can not leave that upper-deck scene aboard COMMONWEALTH without some unanswered queries. Who was the man who hailed COMMONWEALTH with such a sweeping superlative? It was obvious that he knew ships in general and the Fall River Line in particular and that he was widely traveled.

Could he have been associated with the drawings and construction of the COMMONWEALTH—Stevenson Taylor or Warren T. Berry, for instance? Was he an official of the Cramp shipyard or the Quintard Iron Works? Or was he a naval architect who knew that COMMONWEALTH was outstanding in her class? The identity of the man and the fair "Millie" must forever remain unknown, but the influence of his unqualified praise can never die.

No author can honestly say that he alone writes a book. Memories, many of them subconscious, and men, many of whom long since sailed their last voyage, have contributed to this chronicle about the "greatest boat in the world."

Two men who knew every phase of COMMONWEALTH's distinguished career, from beginning to end, almost deserve to be called co-authors. Albert F. Haas, last superintendent of the Fall River Line Repair Shops, Newport, and Captain Norman L. Strickland, COMMONWEALTH's last regular master, have in personal interviews and detailed correspondence given freely of their wide knowledge. Mr. Haas and Captain Strickland have read every word of manuscript, verifying the accuracy of recorded dates, facts, and incidents. To them the author owes an incalculable debt. In addition, the manuscript was diligently read by my friends, Mr. and Mrs. Charles F. Clark, of New Rochelle. My brother John was of especial assistance in going over that part of the manuscript dealing with corporate and financial matters involving Charles W. Morse and the New Haven Railroad.

If there are people more dedicated and helpful than library personnel the author has yet to find them. Extensive use was made of the facilities of the public libraries in Boston, Bridgeport, Fall River, New Haven, New London, New York, Providence, and Yale University. Much valuable data was obtained from old newspaper files in the historical societies in Fall River, New York, and Newport. In all these institutions cooperation was exceptional.

Literally scores of individuals have been of assistance. These include Frank O. Braynard, William King Covell, and Freeman R. Hathaway, past presidents, Steamship Historical Society of America, of which the author is a charter member. Mariners who gave the author precious nuggets of information are Captains John S. Blank, III, Frank H. Bunce, Harold L. Colbeth, Albert Johnson, Chester L. Jordon, Charles T. Snow, and J. L. P. Spooner. Officials of the New Haven Railroad who were outstanding in their cooperation are E. P. Kelly, Arthur G. Koch, Albert E. Spette, Leslie G. Tyler, and John Zeto. Interesting newspaper clippings, some arriving at the most opportune times, came from Herbert W. Alfenburg, Lonsdale, R. I.; George A. Bishop, Fall River; Earl R. Kellogg, Scituate, Mass.; Miss Ella E. Phillips, New London; and Mrs. Edgar H. Pendleton, Providence.

Information of importance was made available for specific chapters by Rear Admiral E. M. Eller (Ret.), Director of Naval History, Washington; Representative Nathaniel Tilden, Scituate, Mass., who allowed the author the use of official documents dealing with the Old Colony Railroad; Herbert A. Charlson, Clerk, United States District Court, Southern District, New York; Mrs. Clara G. Barrows, New London, daughter of Captain Edward R. Geer; John H. Lochhead, The Mariners' Museum, Newport News; Harry E. Ring, Jr., City Clerk, Bath, Maine; Elmer H. Walter, Wireless Operator, Steamer BOSTON, Eastern Steamship Lines in 1924; and Miss Constance M. Winslow, Curator, Fall River Historical Society. Others who made significant contributions are J. Everett Benson, Jersey City; Richard W. Berry, Plainfield, N. J.; Mrs. Thomas M. McGuire, Secretary to the late R. C. Stanley, General Passenger Agent of the Fall River Line; Walter Mitchell III, Tiverton, R. I., Clifford A. Munroe, St. Petersburg; William Rigney, Richmond; Mrs. Thomas H. Stead, New London; and Michael J. Ward, Staten Island.

Once again the author's task was made easy by Mrs. Jean Dillon, of North Arlington, N. J., who faultlessly typed most of the manuscript and efficiently handled much of the correspondence. Several chapters were transcribed by the author's wife, Ruth S. McAdam, and his daughter, Carol C. McAdam.

To all who have been named and to countless others who gave assistance and encouragement, the author expresses his deep gratitude.

R. W. M.

Kearny, New Jersey
May, 1959

CONTENTS

ILLUSTRATIONS

PICTURE CREDITS

Many of the illustrations are photos taken by the author or come from his extensive collection. Other photos are reproduced through the cooperation of the individuals or institutions listed below.

GROUP ONE: From J. Everett Benson—photo of himself; Richard W. Berry—photo of Warren T. Berry; Mrs. F. S. Chapman—photo of J. Howland Gardner; Wm. King Covell—COMMONWEALTH, broadside view; Fall River Historical Society—COMMONWEALTH Barber Shop and Adams Salon; Albert F. Haas—photo of himself, freighter BUNKER HILL, launching of PROVIDENCE, drawing of COMMONWEALTH sidewheel, OLD COLONY at Cramps shipyard, COMMONWEALTH Entrance Lobby, Library, Parlor Bed Room and Empire Salon; John H. Lofland—COMMONWEALTH Grand Stairway; Clifford A. Munroe—PLYMOUTH destroyed by fire; New Haven Railroad—COMMONWEALTH Grand Salon and Grill Room; New York Historical Society—Steamer HARVARD; George

W. Rigby— COMMONWEALTH sidewheel, Grand Salon ceiling, gallery corridor and Dining Room; Capt. J. L. P. Spooner—Newspaper (*Providence Evening Bulletin*), sinking of LARCHMONT; The Society of Naval Architects and Marine Engineers—photo of Stevenson Taylor; Hon. Nathaniel Tilden—Fall River Line Boat Train and parlor car.

GROUP TWO: From the late Mrs. Clara G. Barrows—photo of Capt. Edward R. Geer; *Fall River Line Journal*—photo of Captains Robinson, Barrett, Strickland and Avery; R. Loren Graham—wreck of Steamer HARVARD; Miss M. Hoppé—photo of Hoppé's Fall River Line Orchestra; *Nautical Gazette*—interior photos of YALE and OLD COLONY; New York Public Library—photos of Louis D. Brandeis, J. Pierpont Morgan and Charles W. Morse; George W. Rigby—COMMONWEALTH at Fall River Wharf; William M. Rigney—COMMONWEALTH and LEVIATHAN, North River, New York; Capt. Charles T. Snow—photo of Calvin Austin; Captain Norman L. Strickland—COMMONWEALTH in dry dock; Leslie G. Tyler, New Haven Railroad—photo of Charles S. Mellen.

GROUP THREE: From Ralph M. Arnold—U.S.S. NEW HAMPSHIRE collision damage, PRISCILLA in Cape Cod Canal, COMMONWEALTH landing BOSTON survivors at Newport, Coast Guard towing COMMONWEALTH, tug alongside disabled COMMONWEALTH, COMMONWEALTH at Briggs Wharf, Newport; the late Mrs. Clara G. Barrows—telegram to Capt. E. R. Geer; J. Everett Benson—COMMONWEALTH in dry dock after collision with warship; Edward O. Clark—COMMONWEALTH coaling at Pier 14; Commercial Engraving Company (New London)—BOSTON at Coast Guard base, New London; Wm. King Covell—PLYMOUTH threatened by fire, COMMONWEALTH with stack removed; Fall River Historical Society—loading freight, Pier 14; the late Le Roy N. Frazee—COMMONWEALTH in East River; Carl O. Gustafson—photo of Chief Engineer Peter C. Brooks; Albert F. Haas—COMMONWEALTH, Newport, after collision with warship, COMMONWEALTH stack; *Newport Daily News*—COMMONWEALTH torn from mooring, Briggs Wharf, Newport; R. U. Parker—BOSTON in Cape Cod Canal, BOSTON's Ball Room, NEW YORK's Dining Room; Press Association, Inc.—COMMONWEALTH in storm; William M. Rigney—photo of Capt. Strickland in COMMONWEALTH "middle window"; Mrs. Albert T. Rowland—photo of Captain Fred M. Hamlen; the late Richard C. Stanley—photo of Capt. Strickland greeting diners; The Mariners' Museum—Steamer NEW YORK; Elmer H. Walter—photo of himself.

GROUP FOUR: From Ralph M. Arnold—photo of Chief Engineer John McQueen, COMMONWEALTH Engine Room from upper deck and freight deck; Wm. King Covell—COMMONWEALTH pilothouse, PLYMOUTH's dance floor; R. Loren Graham—Steamers at Pier 14, N. R., New York; Albert F. Haas—COMMONWEALTH parlor room with running water, COMMONWEALTH Engine Room; Miss M. Hoppé—photo of Stanis Hoppé; Clement A. Penrose—PRISCILLA leaving Pier 14, New York; *Providence Journal-Bulletin*—Purser E. J. Flynn on last trip Colonial Line's ARROW; George W. Rigby—COMMONWEALTH bell, two deck views, stripped of furnishings, being towed from Fall River and Fall River Wharf after abandonment of service; the late Richard C. Stanley—stateroom showing running water installation; Mrs. Thomas L. Stead—photo of Purser John F. Ward; the late Theodore E. Steinway—poster announcing the suspension of Fall River Line; Capt. Norman L. Strickland—COMET at Providence dock; *The Boston Herald*—NEW YORK at India Wharf, Boston; The Mariners' Museum—COMMONWEALTH stern carvings; Western Electric Company—Public Address system aboard PRISCILLA.

C H A P T E R   O N E

Millions for Defense!

The potentate of 23 Wall Street accepted Charles W. Morse's declaration of war! Morse, rapidly becoming a coastwise steamship tycoon, audaciously proposed an all-water steamship passenger and express freight service between New York and Boston. J. Pierpont Morgan himself was the board of directors of the New Haven Railroad; native New England was *his* territory. In 1903 he had brought Charles S. Mellen back from the Northern Pacific Railway to head the New Haven. Mellen knew why—Morgan's millions were to expand the New Haven Railroad into a southern New England transportation monopoly. There was to be no competition; travelers venturing from New York to Boston would enrich the New Haven's coffers whether they journeyed by rail, water, or trolley and now came Morse!

Mellen, a New Englander, forty years a railroadman, once second vice president of the New Haven, had hardly been installed in the presidential suite in Elm City's Yellow Building, when the disquieting news came that Charles W. Morse, "energetic son of Bath," had secured control of Maine's important steamboat lines and had his eye on Long Island Sound. The New Haven Railroad, at no little cost, had just completed a merger of Long Island steamboat lines, chief of which was the Old Colony Railroad's Fall River Line. It appeared to be waging a successful battle to scuttle the "blackmail" Enterprise and Joy Lines, which had cut the heart out of New York-New England passenger fares. Pierpont Morgan was in no mood for further armistice or strife involving boat lines.

Since 1897, when a New York newspaperman, long on

ideas but short of capital, had persistently publicized the idea of a direct New York-Boston round Cape Cod passenger service, the New Haven Railroad had been haunted by the fear that a formidable rival to its steamer-rail Fall River Line might someday appear. The Boston Joy Line, with the plodding sidewheeler OLD DOMINION, under Captain William Durkee, had unsuccessfully attempted the "experiment" in 1899 and 1900.

The announcement in May 1905 that Morse had bought for three million dollars the New York-Boston Metropolitan Line freight service and intended to expend four million dollars in building two fast turbine passenger steamers to give deluxe "without change" passenger service imperiled the future of the New Haven's all-rail shore line and its steamer service via Fall River. Wall Street heard that Morse, "the Kennebec River Ice King," had the backing of three hundred million dollars and would not be scared off.

Morgan authorized millions, if necessary, for the defense of Long Island Sound. Telephone wires fairly sizzled between Wall Street and Mellen in the Yellow Building at New Haven; between Mellen and J. Howland Gardner, superintendent of marine construction at the Newport, Rhode Island shops of the Fall River Line; and between Newport and the eminent naval architect, Stevenson Taylor, vice president, Quintard Iron Works, New York. Lights burned all night at Newport and in the Quintard Plant. Plans were quickly shaped—the ultimate in Long Island Sound steamers, surpassing the PRISCILLA in size and splendor, would be built for the Fall River Line. Boston waterfront terminal property would be purchased by the New Haven Railroad; two or possibly three exceptionally fast freight steamers, readily convertible into passenger liners, designed to "beat Morse's flyers into port every morning," would be operated between New York and Boston by a newly formed railroad subsidiary. These ships would drive Morse off the Sound!

Gardner, son of a Fall River Line superintendent, was an

associate of the late George Peirce, designer of several Fall River ships, and knew that he faced one of the greatest challenges ever given a naval architect. In effect, Mellen had instructed, "Build a Fall River steamer greater than the PRISCILLA, more modern than your new PROVIDENCE." The sleek and sumptuous PRISCILLA, then a bit over a decade in service, had received an accolade from an expert only a few days before. Captain George L. Norton in a *Marine Journal* editorial had saluted the PRISCILLA as "a dream in naval architecture." "No handsomer steamboat floats salt water" penned Norton. "She suggests the query whether those who knew the late George Peirce, her designer, fully appreciated his great ability." How casually the white-haired Mellen, sitting hard by his locomotives and box cars in New Haven, had said, "Build a greater PRISCILLA!" The very audacity of Morgan and Mellen! They were implying that George Peirce's masterpiece could be relegated to a secondary role on the Atlantic Coast.[1]

Stevenson Taylor, "the grand old man of marine engineering," joined Gardner and the technical staff of Newport Shops in almost daily conferences. Taylor had started as an apprentice at the North River Iron Works of Fletcher, Harrison and Company in 1864. He, too, had been closely associated with George Peirce and was the right-hand man of "Uncle Andy" Fletcher at the Hoboken plant of the famous W. & A. Fletcher Company, which had considered PRISCILLA its honor ship. Taylor knew everything about the Fall River sidewheelers. He had designed the massive beam engines for the PILGRIM and the PURITAN[2] and the powerful compound engine of the PRISCILLA. When Peirce died suddenly in his Newport home, the very night he completed the draft of the construction contract for the PROVIDENCE, Taylor was named the Fall River Line's consulting engineer. "Build greater than the PRISCILLA!" A formidable assignment, indeed.

[1] *Seaboard Magazine,* June 28, 1894 said, "PRISCILLA is the greatest steamboat now or ever known."

[2] PURITAN had largest beam engine ever built.

Seven men, conscious that something big was afoot, met in Gardner's Newport office. Flanking Gardner and Taylor were the Line's general manager, Captain Jacob W. Miller, an Annapolis graduate; Warren T. Berry, who was Taylor's nephew as well as the superintendent of the Quintard Iron Works; and a trio of Newport Shops technicians: William S. Rogers, foreman joiner, Albert F. Haas, and J. Everett Benson, draftsmen. Pungently Gardner cited the railroad's determination that "Morse must not encroach on our passenger business." He outlined the New Haven's command and demand for the construction of the Sound's most magnificent passenger ship in addition to the fastest freighters ever known in the United States.

In no way minimizing the problems involved, Taylor gave heart to the group by pointing out that A. Cary Smith, contemporary designer of the Sound's popular twin-screw vessels, had actually beaten himself in design. "Everybody said Cary Smith's RICHARD PECK was absolutely unbeatable when she came out in 1892," recalled the white-haired naval architect. "Two years later," he continued, "he brought out the CITY OF LOWELL . . ."

Gardner impetuously broke in, "I don't like to interrupt you, Steve; but let's not forget our sidewheeler PURITAN was a real match for the PECK, and the PRISCILLA beat the LOWELL when they were both brand new." [3]

With a chuckle Taylor said, "Howland, your father never forgot that race and Brady, of the Norwich Line, never forgave the PRISCILLA." Turning to the group he continued, "But as I was saying, before Howland started racing steamboats, Smith came along with the CHESTER W. CHAPIN, the best of the three. Gentlemen, let's get busy and beat ourselves!"

If only a tape recording device had existed in 1905! An

[3] *Priscilla of Fall River,* Roger Williams McAdam: Stephen Daye Press, 1956, p. 76.

opportunity to listen in on the animated conversations at Newport Shops as the "build greater than PRISCILLA" doubts and difficulties were analyzed by the experts would be edifying. Safety, spaciousness, and speed were the fundamental requirements for the proposed Fall River queen. In view of the more than right-angle turn inside Borden Flats Lighthouse, Fall River, extremely hazardous in a southerly gale and a flood tide, and of the confined channel rounding Newport's Naval Torpedo Station, could the new ship be longer than the PRISCILLA? How much longer? Because staterooms made the money how could dozens more be built? Morse's plan to bring the speediest coastal liners to the Sound meant that the new steamer must be a twenty knot vessel. Should the sidewheel type of propulsion be abandoned in favor of twin screws or turbines? The serious fire, starting in the cotton cargo, which had virtually destroyed the freighter MOHAWK[4] in the Sound a few months before had aroused Mellen's fear "of a disaster on one of the great big tinder boxes running on the Sound." The fire hazard must be conquered!

The conferees were surprised and raised their eyes as one man when Gardner ejaculated, "I see red every time I think of this new steamer!" Noting their astonishment Gardner explained, "Yes, red! I mean fire, gentlemen. You all remember that I just happened to be on the north shore of Long Island when the abandoned MOHAWK drifted ashore. I got there and handled the salvage. I wouldn't allow the tugs to put a stream of water on her; I figured that would ruin the hull and engines. Even though she was blazing like the fires of hell we were able to pull her off the beach and tow her to New London. She burned in the harbor for days. Because we hadn't put water on the fire a lot of the steel plating, angles, beams, frames, and stringers were faired and replaced. But that disaster convinced

[4] November 17, 1904. Freighter BOSTON, Capt. M. I. Brightman, rescued crew of twenty-seven; one life lost.

me that as long as our passenger ships have to carry cotton to Fall River we are running a big risk. Gentlemen, there must be no more MOHAWKS!"

The pros and cons of the new sidewheeler PROVIDENCE, rapidly nearing completion, were weighed by the hour. She had been designed by George Peirce as a replacement for the PILGRIM, and especially for winter service. Forty-three feet shorter than the PRISCILLA, she had practically the same number of staterooms. This had been accomplished by a more ingenious arrangement and a greater use of the upper deck. The PROVIDENCE was making the headlines—she had a telephone in every stateroom and a new type of ventilating system.

To hundreds of passengers the telephone was indeed a mysterious gadget. Few in 1905 had telephones in their homes. Therefore, elaborate instructions had to be posted in all PROVIDENCE staterooms. "Speak clearly and in not too loud a tone of voice," and "Be sure to place the receiver back on the hook" were among the suggestions. Ah, but the convenience of the contrivance! It was no longer necessary to ring a bell to summon a porter to fetch ice water or hot water for shaving or to find out from the purser when the train left for Barnstable. You simply spoke into a black box on the wall and seconds later your desires were fulfilled. That was the Fall River Line for you—years ahead of the times!

Discussions concerning the new steamer inevitably centered on main deck and upper deck plans. PRISCILLA's dining room was on the main deck; that of the PROVIDENCE, below the main deck, admittedly unsatisfactory in a steamer for summer service. The upper deck cabin on the PROVIDENCE extended practically the full length of the steamer. On the new ship why not make the dining room the crowning feature by placing it on the upper deck? That would afford space on the main deck, aft of the entrance lobby, for a lounge and for additional staterooms. Well, why not? The *haut monde,* a phrase aptly describing the patronage of the Fall River Line, would certainly appreciate a "roof garden" atmosphere while dining.

Albert F. Haas and J. Everett Benson, who worked on the plans, have clear recollections of the complex problem of locating the dining room. The great weight and height would alter the steamer's center of gravity. The dining room and kitchen would have to be carried on a steel structure and by heavy columns. The PRISCILLA was used at Newport for testing the proposed dining room. Canvas-covered wooden pillars were hauled aboard and erected against the PRISCILLA's papier maché decorated ceiling to indicate the appearance and feasibility of such supports. Haas, who made all the computations at the Newport Shops, designed a steel hull on a fifty-five foot beam to carry the additional weight. Masts, characteristic of all the other Fall River passenger steamers, were eliminated.

Along with the dining room discussion there was much debate concerning the new vessel's mode of propulsion. Every Fall River passenger steamer from the pioneer BAY STATE of 1847 had been a paddler. Since 1875 the development of the propeller had been noteworthy. The single-screw Stonington liners MAINE and NEW HAMPSHIRE and the New Haven Line's twin-screw flyer RICHARD PECK, all built in 1892, had proved economical and popular. Morse's New York-Boston round the Cape ships were to be turbine driven like the new GOVERNOR COBB. E. H. B. Anderson, representing C. A. Parsons of Britain, suggested a triple-screw turbine drive with a speed of about nineteen knots. Points of view met head on. General Manager Miller strongly favored continuation of the sidewheel motive power and stressed the word "power." Too many reports of near collisions with yawing coal and lumber schooners came across his desk; the backing power of the paddlers was a distinct asset on the Sound where fog was a common hazard. Taylor contributed the strong argument that nowhere in the world had the sidewheeler reached such perfection as on Long Island Sound. Gardner and Haas agreed that for the Fall River *passenger* service the paddle wheel vessel was quieter and steadier, factors of no mean importance in night service. The safeguard to the hull against collision damage given by the overhanging guards was recognized by all. Furthermore, the wide guards permitted the commodious assembly rooms and tiers of staterooms expected by the traveling public on a Fall River steamer.

When everything had been talked out, Haas was commissioned to draft plans for a sidewheeler 455 feet, 2 inches long, 94 feet, 7 inches beam over guards. She would be the world's largest sidewheeler, exceeded in history only by the fabulous GREAT EASTERN, of 1858, 693 feet long and 120 feet wide. (As detailed in the next chapter, Newport Shops were also designing three fast "opposition to Morse" freighters. Here the twin screw and triple screw were overwhelmingly favored.)

The first three months of 1906 were nerve-wracking at Newport Shops. Five new steamers of different types were being designed; five vessels were berthed there undergoing repairs. To complete a major overhaul, much of the triple expansion inclined engine had been removed from PLYMOUTH's innards and placed on the dock. An "experiment" was taking place on a new freighter of the MOHAWK[5] class. A Grinnell dry pipe automatic fire sprinkler system was being installed aboard her. Night after night Albert Haas came to his home on Newport Avenue weary in mind and body. On the evening of March 26 he retired early.

Deep in slumber, Haas had a vague sense that Newport's fire whistle was blasting an alarm. Partially aroused, he counted mechanically—then came awake with a start: the private box number 15 at the shops was sounding. A glance out the window confirmed that a major conflagration was starting. Newport's fire whistle was shrieking a second alarm. It was the dead of night—2:30 A.M.—but the western sky was lurid. Tossing on his clothing, Haas rushed toward the waterfront. Already he could see flames roaring up the 150-foot high

[5] The PEQUONNOCK, 1906.
[6] Flames seen by eastbound PILGRIM off Point Judith.

wooden hoisting shears:[6] "My God, what are we up against?" he asked himself as he hastened toward the harbor. "The LOWELL is right next to the PLYMOUTH; if it spreads we're going to lose everything—the PRISCILLA, the PURITAN, and the NAUGATUCK."

Racing madly across Washington Street, the air filled with cracklings and crashings, the draftsman headed straight for the office where the computations and plans for the new steamers were in the fireproof vault. Close by was a raging inferno. The tall shears were a flaming torch; the million dollar PLYMOUTH was a mass of flame; the side of the CITY OF LOWELL was blazing fiercely but the tugs C. T. MORSE and SOLICITOR had lines aboard and were pulling her out into the stream; the pier shed was on fire; embers were falling all over the waterfront. With the assistance of shop employees arriving from all directions, Gardner and Haas began removing precious documents, paintings, and ship models.

Gardner, recalling the lack of permanent hull damage when the MOHAWK's superstructure was allowed to burn, pleaded with the Newport firemen to divert all streams from the doomed PLYMOUTH. Quick work by the tugs had extinguished the fire threatening the LOWELL and had towed the PRISCILLA and the other steamers to safety. PLYMOUTH's chief engineer, John McElvie, stumbled into view and told Gardner a harrowing tale of escape. The fire, starting in the glory hole, cause unknown, had been discovered by the watchman at 2:25 A.M. and was out of control before effective action could be taken. The engineering crew of thirteen men, two of whom were forced to leap into the harbor, barely got ashore. One was missing and presumed trapped aboard.

Dawn brought the devastation and ruin into sharp focus. The PLYMOUTH, her steel hull reddened by the terrific heat, was a gutted wreck. Her smokestack made a lonely thrust into the sky because her cabins and decks had disappeared. Gardner and Haas were grateful that so much of PLYMOUTH's engine had been removed from the vessel before the fire.

Fortunately, the main shop buildings had escaped serious damage so work could continue without interruption.

Two imperatives faced Gardner and Taylor before the PLYMOUTH embers had cooled. Added to all the conferences about the new ships was the unexpected question of rebuilding or replacing the destroyed PLYMOUTH. Most important was the stark fact that a shipboard fire could nullify all other safety measures. The fire sprinkler system being installed on the new freighter was no longer an "experiment." Since examination showed that the PLYMOUTH's hull and engine could be used in reconstruction, it was decided that she would serve as the laboratory for testing fire prevention and protective equipment to be incorporated in the new deluxe steamer.

Pioneers were now at work. Drawings for the reconstructed PLYMOUTH were prepared at Newport Shops. The steamer was to be divided into three sections by fire-resisting bulkheads extending from the keel to the upper deck. Fireproof doors were fitted into passageways and large sliding doors were planned for the freight deck. A complete fire sprinkler system was included. The rebuilt PLYMOUTH was the first ship known to have fire bulkhead protection and the first passenger liner with a fire sprinkler system. On August 12, 1907, the new PLYMOUTH made her first appearance "with colors flying from every flagstaff." Her fireproof features were widely hailed.

When the contract for the new passenger liner was executed with the Quintard Iron Works on October 15, 1906, a sprinkler system consisting of eighteen hundred Grinnell automatic outlets was specified. In addition, plans called for sixty-five fire hydrants throughout the steamer. She, too, was to have fire bulkheads extending through all decks to the dome, dividing the vessel into three compartments. An iron bulkhead across the upper deckhouse was provided forward of the kitchen.

While Quintard's had the contract for the complete ship, the hull was being built in Philadelphia by William Cramp and

Sons Ship and Engine Building Company. Thus were joined two of the greatest construction firms in American nautical history. The Quintard Iron Works had been established in 1863 by George W. Quintard, son-in-law of Charles Morgan, "father of coastwise shipping in the United States," founder of the famous Morgan Line and the Morgan Iron Works, New York. The Cramp Company, organized in 1830 by William Cramp, was "a shipyard whose history is entwined with America."

In a few months Quintard let marine reporters know that they were constructing a new sidewheeler "which in grandeur, elegance, and completeness will eclipse anything ever before attempted for service on Long Island Sound." The boast was made that "the internal arrangements of the new Fall River Line steamer will prove the most perfect ever placed at the disposal of the traveling public." But Quintard was not getting all the headlines. From the rival W. & A. Fletcher Company in Hoboken came equally enthusiastic boasts about the turbine liners being built there for Charles W. Morse's new Sound service. The public relations boys were having a field day.

Autumn of 1907 saw copious splashes of printer's ink and salt water. Morse's new HARVARD made her first passenger-carrying voyage New York to Boston on Monday evening, September 9—and almost came to grief! At dangerous Hell Gate there was a lively five minutes. Attempting to avoid a tug flanked by two noncooperative car floats, the HARVARD was forced to swing off her course. Dodging and twisting in the tortuous passage, it was feared the HARVARD might rip her hull on the jagged rocks. She did touch lightly, but a thorough examination of her bottom showed only slight damage and after a short delay she steamed off toward her destination. Mellen and Morgan were not overcome with joy to learn that "because of popular demand" the HARVARD had inaugurated the new Metropolitan Line "express service" a week earlier than officially announced. Nine days later the blue-interiored

YALE left Boston and made the hazardous 337-mile run "'round the Cape and over the shoals" in less than the scheduled fifteen hours. She was a quarter of an hour ahead of her 8 A.M. docking time in New York. In deep water the YALE roared along at better than twenty knots. The HARVARD was also the marine reporters' delight; nightly she was showing that the timetable which called for a fifteen-hour passage dock to dock was an affront to her power. The papers were full of tales about nautical speed—the Cunard liner LUSITANIA was also demolishing records.

A month later (October 10, 1907) Mellen's tub thumpers had their inning and took full advantage of their time at bat. When little Kathryn Mellen broke a bottle of champagne against the towering bow and the giant sidewheeler took to the water at Cramps, the occasion was described as "'a momentous launching in the history of American shipbuilding." A large party came from New York by special train to witness the Philadelphia christening. One of the guests was Calvin Austin, of the Consolidated Steamship Company, an ally of Charles W. Morse. In view of later developments in the bitterly competitive New England transportation era his wangling an invitation must be recorded as a tribute to the atmosphere surrounding the city of brotherly love. Typewriters and linotypes clattered merrily. There was column after column about the Fall River Line's "largest steamboat in the world." "A steamer, whose decorations will surpass anything previously attempted"; "a steamer with the look of great strength and seaworthy qualities." Such was the launching of the great new COMMONWEALTH.

When Kathryn Mellen gave the name COMMONWEALTH to the big paddler a Fall River Line tradition was smashed into as many fragments as the beribboned bottle. Forty years earlier, Jim Fisk's lavish PROVIDENCE had been the talk of the nation. Then had come a series of passenger ships which had given honor to the letter P—PILGRIM, PURITAN, PLYMOUTH, PRISCILLA, and a second PROVIDENCE. (The name COMMON-

WEALTH had originally been assigned to one of the New Haven Railroad's new freight boats which instead was christened BUNKER HILL.)

An exploding box of matches gave young Norman L. Strickland, a Fall River Line apprentice, the big break of his five years of service. The COMMONWEALTH was ready to be delivered by the Cramps late in June 1908. Quartermaster Harry Anderson had been one of the pair of helmsmen given the honor of going to Philadelphia to steer the new liner up the Jersey coast. Just before the great day, Anderson severely burned his hand when a container of matches flared up. Captain Henry O. Nickerson, major domo at New York headquarters, dispatched an order to Captain William B. Appleby, freighter NASHUA, relieving his quartermaster, Strickland, for a special assignment.

Special assignment? It was a command performance! Strickland, but a lad, was being given man's work—his steady hands were to help deliver the two-million-dollar COMMONWEALTH from the builders to the Fall River Line. Strickland never forgot his first glimpse of the giantess which he was to command a quarter of a century later.[7] "She's got no masts!" was his ejaculation on glimpsing her at the Cramp yard.

On Saturday noon, June 20, the COMMONWEALTH left Philadelphia under command of Captain "Handsome Harry" Barrett, an old sidewheeler man from the Stonington service, who had been handling the railroad's dashing new freighter MASSACHUSETTS, New York to Boston, for some weeks previously. Besides a coastwise pilot, the navigational board of directors comprised Samuel Crocker, first pilot, senior grade; Daniel Grinnell, first pilot, junior grade; the veteran Jacob Flye and young Strickland, quartermasters; and John V. Sheldon, chief engineer. The weather was clear as the COMMONWEALTH churned down the Delaware River, but fog curtained the onward progress at Lewes and Captain Barrett anchored for the night.

[7] Summer of 1933.

Then the fun began. There were some three hundred company officials and guests aboard with Orlando H. Taylor, general passenger agent, as host. Corks popped in salute to the COMMONWEALTH as the gala dinner was deftly served. It was the first time that Strickland had ever tasted champagne. At 4:15 Sunday morning the COMMONWEALTH upped anchor and left the Delaware Breakwater for New York. There was no sea running as the liner made a smooth passage past the Jersey beaches. Captain Barrett and Chief Engineer Sheldon made no attempt to let her out for any speed record. She arrived in New York's upper harbor at 4:30 Sunday afternoon and berthed at Pier 40, North River, the Norwich Line terminal, to receive movable furniture and other equipment. Gardner, Taylor, Berry, and other officials, their trained eyes taking in every phase of her operation, were certain that they had built a steamer "greater than PRISCILLA," the craft so soon to relinquish her title as flagship of the line.

The workers at the shipyard were proud of her, too. Years later one of the Cramp[8] staff, who had worked at the busy Philadelphia yard on the construction of battleships, ocean liners, and tugboats, voted the COMMONWEALTH "the most interesting of all the vessels built at Cramps. Except for the keel she had not a straight line. The sheer line and shape of the decks were all of beautiful parabola curves."

On Saturday, June 27, the COMMONWEALTH graced the waters of Long Island Sound for the first time. Her daylight run to Newport made headlines. According to the *New York Herald* she "proved herself the fastest steamer on the Sound." This sweeping claim was predicated on a reported speed of 22½ knots sustained during a four-hour stretch. Engineers on Morse's twin flyers HARVARD and YALE snorted at such bragging. They were eager to meet the new vessel alone somewhere on a dark night. Privately, however, they admitted the COMMONWEALTH's one-hundred-ton sidewheels were not mere ornaments.

[8] Harry B. Etten.

The advertising copywriters for both services filled the columns of the travel pages with blurbs. A trip on the Sound became the great adventure of the time. In the Fall River Line space, jubilation was the keynote. At a fare of $3.65 (plus stateroom and meals) the Fall River Line was *"the best way to go to Boston."*[9] Bold type immediately below exulted, "In splendor and magnificence the new steamer COMMONWEALTH outrivals any vessel in American waters." There was nothing modest about the Metropolitan Line's announcement, either. The "all-the-way-by-water" route (a sly jab at the early morning boat train, Fall River to Boston) served by the "fast and luxurious triple screw turbine steamships HARVARD and YALE" was termed *"the finest water trip in the world."*

There was unrestrained rejoicing and cheering when the eagerly awaited COMMONWEALTH came to the Spindle City on Wednesday, July 1. Hours before her scheduled arrival from Newport, people had preempted the vantage spots along the Fall River waterfront. Every inch of space on sprawling Fall River Wharf was taken. Suddenly those keenest of vision sent up the shout, "Here she comes!" The glistening white steamer, gayly bedecked, was seen turning into Mount Hope Bay for the first time. Whistles from the scores of cotton mills and a volley from the cannon mounted on the Staples Coal Company wharf released thousands of decibels. Ships in the harbor clanged and tooted. "Never before in the history of Fall River was a steamer accorded a more royal salute," said the *Fall River Herald News.*

One man in particular must have been deeply moved by conflicting emotions as he witnessed a simple ceremony. Stevenson Taylor watched sadly, but gladly too, as the PURITAN of 1889, first Fall River liner to exceed four hundred feet in length, lying in the south berth, saluted the new COMMONWEALTH and pulled out for Newport. It was not the ordinary

[9] Fall River Line was owned by New Haven Railroad which ran trains, New York and Boston.

substitution of steamer routine; PURITAN's status was changed in the twinkling of an eye. Two decades before, the PURITAN was "the largest and in every respect the finest steamer of her class ever built." She had been one of Taylor's first big jobs at Fletcher's. Surely the PURITAN, harboring the largest beam engine ever built, not yet old by shipbuilding standards, was not already shorn of her queenly status! But she was—the bitter words had come—"The PURITAN will lay up at Newport as a spare boat." And he, Stevenson Taylor, was an accessory to her dethronement!

Captain George H. Williamson, another Stonington Line veteran taken into the Fall River Line family by the New Haven Railroad's merger of the Sound lines, came from the PRISCILLA to command the new flagship. The belief that Williamson was awed and even a bit fearful of COMMONWEALTH's bulk and power seems verified by the frequency with which he anchored the big craft on foggy nights and his extreme caution in New York's jam-packed East River. Solidly booked for the maiden voyage, the COMMONWEALTH left Fall River Wharf amid huzzas. Fog christened the new steamer on her way to Newport, giving the whistle a good workout and Newporters an earful of stentorian blasts. Later the thick mist vanished, enabling the Point Judith life saving station to log the passing of the "speediest and most costly Sound vessel on her initial trip." How Morse must have winced at the repeated newspaper references to the COMMONWEALTH's speed and cost!

But Fall River had another big day coming up. The need to press the COMMONWEALTH into immediate service to accommodate the heavy July Fourth holiday travel made a public inspection at her home port impossible prior to her maiden voyage. That took place on Thursday, July 9, from three to five o'clock in the afternoon. Nearly 5000 persons passed over the gangplank. If any came to scoff they were a decided minority on leaving the steamer. After viewing the paintings by R. Benvenuti and George M. Carpenter; the two-deck Vene-

Metropolitan Steamship's Neptune, New York-Boston. Note auxiliary power

Early view of historic Fall River Line Boat Train

Old Colony Railroad's ornate Fall River Boat Train parlor car Pilgrim

Boston Joy Line's OLD DOMINION

Deck scene, OLD DOMINION

Launching of 1905 PROVIDENCE at Quincy, Mass.

Safeguarding new COMMONWEALTH against disaster concerned her designers

Left: PLYMOUTH, swept by fire, 1906

Below: Tragic loss of LARCHMONT, 1907

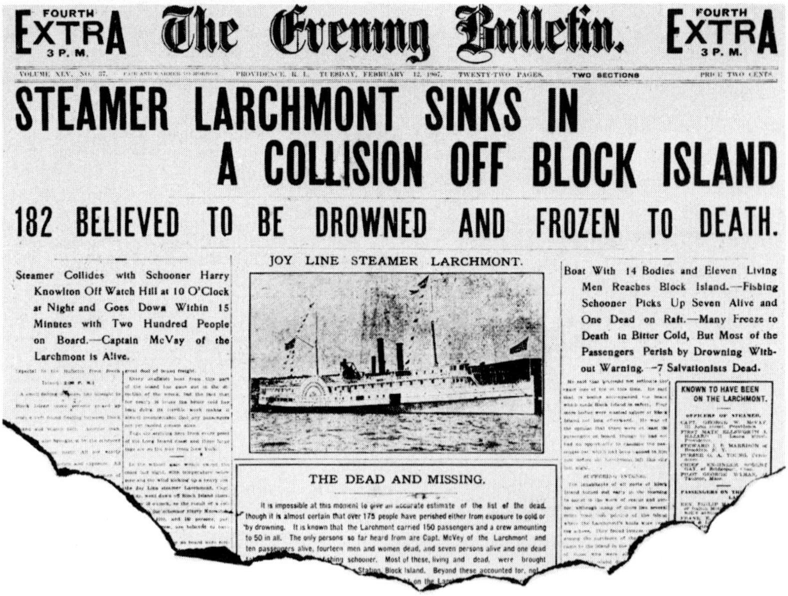

FOURTH EXTRA 3 P. M. **The Evening Bulletin.** FOURTH EXTRA 3 P. M.

PROVIDENCE, R. I., TUESDAY, FEBRUARY 12, 1907. TWENTY-TWO PAGES. TWO SECTIONS PRICE TWO CENTS

STEAMER LARCHMONT SINKS IN A COLLISION OFF BLOCK ISLAND

182 BELIEVED TO BE DROWNED AND FROZEN TO DEATH.

Steamer Collides with Schooner Harry Knowlton Off Watch Hill at 10 O'Clock at Night and Goes Down Within 15 Minutes with Two Hundred People on Board.—Captain McVay of the Larchmont is Alive.

JOY LINE STEAMER LARCHMONT.

Boat With 14 Bodies and Eleven Living Men Reaches Block Island.—Fishing Schooner Picks Up Seven Alive and One Dead on Raft.—Many Freeze to Death in Bitter Cold, But Most of the Passengers Perish by Drowning Without Warning.—7 Salvationists Dead.

KNOWN TO HAVE BEEN ON THE LARCHMONT.

THE DEAD AND MISSING.

It is impossible at this moment to give an accurate estimate of the list of the dead, though it is almost certain that over 175 people have perished either from exposure to cold or by drowning. It is known that the Larchmont carried 150 passengers and a crew amounting to 50 in all. The only persons so far heard from are Capt. McVey of the Larchmont and ten passengers alive, fourteen men and women dead, and seven persons alive and one dead ... fishing schooner. Most of these, living and dead, were brought ... Station, Block Island. Beyond these accounted for, not ... on the Larchmont ...

Top: Warren T. Berry (left) and Albert F. Haas
Center: J. Howland Gardner
Below: Stevenson Taylor (left) and J. Everett Benson

DESIGNERS OF COMMONWEALTH

Fast freighter MASSACHUSETTS with "bone in her teeth"

Morse's HARVARD set speed marks on both coasts

COMMONWEALTH, a twenty-knot sidewheeler

Freighter BUNKER HILL had many a "race" with HARVARD

THE NAUTICAL ROYALTY

Freighter Old Colony taking form at Cramp's shipyard

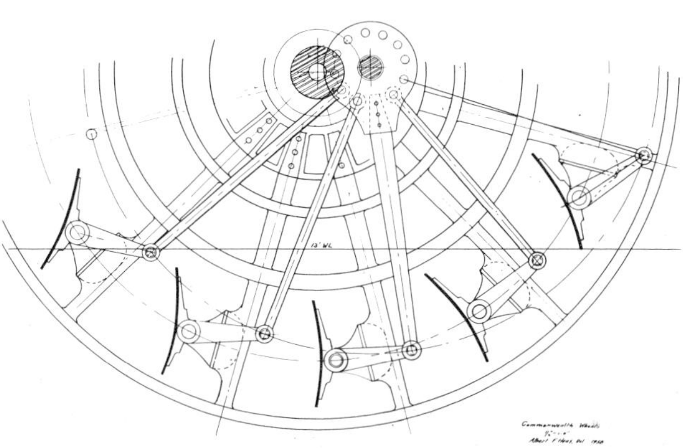

A Commonwealth sidewheel. Drawing by Albert F. Haas

Powerful sidewheel, port side.
Each wheel weighed one hundred tons

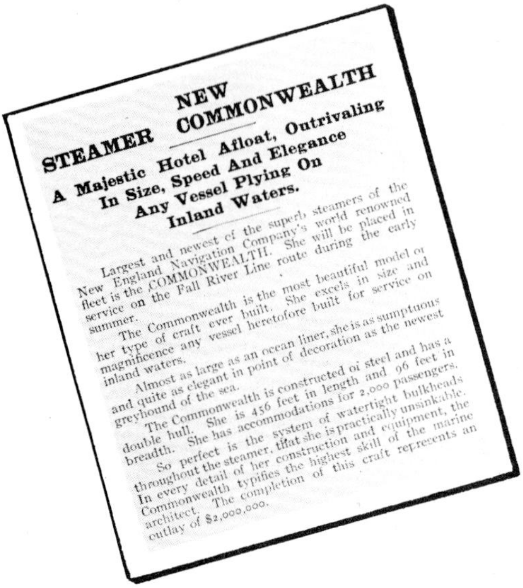

STEAMER NEW COMMONWEALTH

A Majestic Hotel Afloat, Outrivaling In Size, Speed And Elegance Any Vessel Plying On Inland Waters.

Largest and newest of the superb steamers of the New England Navigation Company's world renowned fleet is the COMMONWEALTH. She will be placed in service on the Fall River Line route during the early summer.

The Commonwealth is the most beautiful model of her type of craft ever built. She excels in size and magnificence any vessel heretofore built for service on inland waters.

Almost as large as an ocean liner, she is as sumptuous and quite as elegant in point of decoration as the newest greyhound of the sea.

The Commonwealth is constructed oi steel and has a double hull. She is 456 feet in length and 96 feet in breadth. She has accommodations for 2,000 passengers.

So perfect is the system of watertight bulkheads throughout the steamer, that she is practically unsinkable. In every detail of her construction and equipment, the Commonwealth typifies the highest skill of the marine architect. The completion of this craft represents an outlay of $2,000,000.

Lobby—Modern English style, oak

Library—Louis XVI period, old ivory embellished with gold

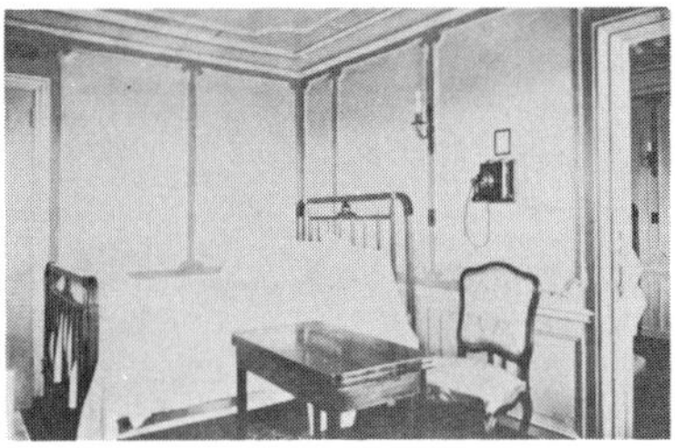

Louis XV bedroom

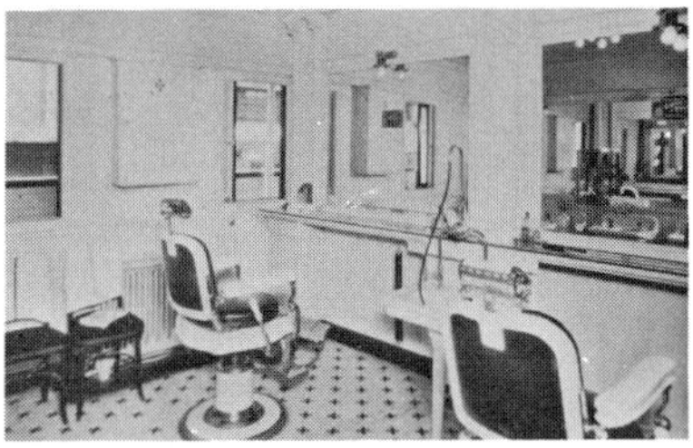

Barber shop

Detail of COMMONWEALTH's Grand Salon ceiling featuring old galleons and sea emblems

Two-deck Venetian-Gothic Grand Salon

Empire Salon—Honduras mahogany, gold ornamentation

Top: Grand stairway. Left: gallery corridor. Right: Adams Salon (card room). Brilliantly illuminated upper deck Dining Room seated 300; "Roof Garden" (Grill Room)

tian-Gothic Grand Saloon; the mahogany and gold Empire Saloon; the green-panelled Adams Saloon; the Louis XVI dining room "on the roof"; the English Renaissance Café, not to mention the office for the public stenographer, the telephone central exchange and the library from which passengers could borrow books, the Fall River folk came ashore enraptured that this great liner was their very own.

Veteran Fall River Line patrons noticed two basic changes before they had taken one hundred steps. Every lounge room and passageway on the COMMONWEALTH differed in architectural style, woodwork, and color scheme. Gone was the familiar red and gold carpet, a Fall River Line trademark for years. Not one yard of it was observed on the COMMONWEALTH. Instead, the new liner's commodious apartments had varying carpet designs in red, mulberry red, green, and two-tone brown gold.

Seven different architectural styles, a decided departure from the norm, were built into the COMMONWEALTH. All of the interior cabinet work, furnishings, and decorations were executed by the Pottier and Stymus Company of New York, under the personal supervision of W. P. Stymus. So great was the interest in the new steamer's interior design that the magazine *The New York Architect* brought out a special illustrated COMMONWEALTH edition, which commended the ship as "an extraordinary success from every point of view."

The COMMONWEALTH, sold out almost every night, was proving herself a speedy craft. But for months nobody knew "officially" just how fast she could paddle. The steamer had been put into regular service immediately on completion and because of the continued heavy travel "could not be spared for a trial trip" until Saturday, November 14. That day, after unloading her passengers and freight at Fall River, progressive speed trials were run over the government course in Narragansett Bay to determine the indicated horsepower at various speeds and a comparison with the data obtained from model experiments at the government tank in Washington. The course was one knot long with a depth of water from twenty to twenty-three fathoms.

Under the personal supervision of J. Howland Gardner, eleven runs were made, starting at 10:45 A.M. and continuing until 2:30 P.M. During the first runs the tide was flood, changing to ebb at about 12:45 P.M. The first four runs were at 29.77 revolutions per minute, speed 20.05 knots (23.09 statute miles), indicated horsepower 12,000.

Speaking before the Society of Naval Architects and Marine Engineers, in New York, after the tests, Stevenson Taylor pointed out one decided advantage of the sidewheeler on a crowded marine highway like Long Island Sound. "On the trial trip of the COMMONWEALTH," he said, "while running a little over nineteen miles per hour, the signal came to the engine room, and progress was absolutely stopped in one minute and ten seconds. I know of no other type of vessel of similar displacement with which that could be done."

Early in 1909 Gardner eagerly scanned a report received from the railroad's accounting department in Mellen's Yellow Building at New Haven. Reaching into his desk, the superintendent of marine construction quickly ran his finger down a column of figures. His expression plainly showed that he liked what he found. He rang for Albert Haas. When the genial draftsman entered the private office, Gardner joyously greeted him, "Albert, the traveling public has proved to my satisfaction that COMMONWEALTH is accepted as greater than PRISCILLA. Look at the Fall River Line carryings for 1894 when the PRISCILLA first came out late in June–364,582 passengers that year. But even though we were bucking Morse's new direct steamers, our first year shows 371,684. Mellen certainly ought to be delighted!"

Late in February the COMMONWEALTH had a new distinction. So many New Englanders were traveling to Washington for the inauguration of President William Howard Taft that all staterooms on the PLYMOUTH were engaged a month ahead.

Many Bay State notables begged for reservations to go in fitting style on the flagship, laid up for the winter in Newport. Therefore the COMMONWEALTH was placed in special service out of Fall River on Sunday evening, February 28, 1909, and sailed to New York completely sold out. The same night the PLYMOUTH transported from Fall River three companies of the Sixth Massachusetts Infantry and two troops of cavalry, Washington bound.

C H A P T E R   T W O

The Year of Nautical Royalty

Early in the twentieth century a vexed marine reporter penned this plaint: "The importance of launching fine ships is often overlooked. Perhaps the daily newspapers could be induced to give their readers less tiresome yarns on golf, baseball, prize fights, divorces, and murders and devote more space to ships, which play so important a part in world progress."

Seven years later the same writer had little cause to be downhearted; he was rushing from shipyard to shipyard recording launching festivities. The metropolitan dailies in picture and text were giving plenty of space to "the importance of launching fine ships." Within weeks, six of the most notable steam vessels ever known were set afloat at American east coast yards. The vigor of the competition between Morgan's New Haven Railroad and Morse's Metropolitan Line made 1907 the year of nautical royalty!

In rapid succession the massive steel hulls of the coastal liners, YALE, HARVARD, MASSACHUSETTS, BUNKER HILL, OLD COLONY and COMMONWEALTH—a glorious sextette—slid into the water. What ships they were! What records for regularity and speed they established in peacetime! What yeoman service they rendered in global conflicts! Merchantmen and admirals revered them. Do not think for one moment that these beloved craft were mere cockleshell short-haul overnight steamers. During World War I, five of them served conspicuously thousands of miles away from the home waters they were designed to ply.

Following three highly successful seasons on Morse's New York-Boston route, the twin flyers HARVARD and YALE had a new "round the Cape" experience of gigantic proportion—one of the great sagas of American maritime history. The erstwhile Sound liners coursed down the South American coast and rounded Cape Horn to gain new fame. Operating all year round[1] between San Francisco and Los Angeles, the collegiate duo set Pacific coast speed marks and became even more popular than they had been on the Atlantic coast. Then World War I called them into service. Both came back to the Atlantic, steamed to Southampton and transported over 368,000 troops across the English Channel.[2] YALE, as Navy's GREYHOUND, was in Pacific World War II service.

MASSACHUSETTS, BUNKER HILL, and OLD COLONY, built in 1907 to rival Morse's HARVARD and YALE, were the "fastest freight steamers built for any service." That was distinction enough to list them among the greats. Subsequently converted into passenger liners, they proved worthy successors to the HARVARD and the YALE, between New York and Boston. To help foil the Kaiser the trio were drafted by the Navy. Altered and renamed, the popular MASSACHUSETTS and her sister, BUNKER HILL, engaged in back-breaking, gruelling work as mine layers in the North Sea. Years later, on the "day of infamy," J. Howland Gardner's MASSACHUSETTS, then Navy's OGLALA, was a victim of the sneak attack on Pearl Harbor.[3] The OLD COLONY was a British hospital ship in World War I. Memorable names in the dramatic history of American maritime achievements are these Sound liners of 1907-08!

Although she performed no direct war service, the side-wheeler COMMONWEALTH brought glamour to the Sound and ranks with the elite. Indeed, on one of her early trips into Newport her presence set the waterfront aglow. She came scraping along ancient Long Wharf with such force and speed

[1] Ran only in the summer, New York and Boston.

[2] *Famous American Ships,* Frank O. Braynard, Hastings House, 1956, p. 142.

[3] *The Old Fall River Line,* Roger Williams McAdam, Stephen Daye Press, 1955, p. 241.

that the resultant friction set the piles afire and the Newport Fire Department had to be summoned. But her power did more than set piers ablaze. An early passenger, a dour Scot, was an expert in matters nautical. Dr. John Inglis, of Glasgow, one of Great Britain's best-known paddleboat designers, after a night on the COMMONWEALTH, said that he was "extremely enthusiastic" over her performance. From a Scot that is rhapsody! Soon after the new rival ships reached the Sound, the publication *Master, Mate and Pilot* inaugurated a monthly series entitled "Notable American Steamers," covering ocean, coastal, and river vessels. COMMONWEALTH placed third; YALE was eighth in the series.[4] How the steering-wheel guild tore into those rankings and omissions during the night watches!

J. Pierpont Morgan became a director of the New Haven Railroad in 1892. It was a period of rail consolidation and frenzied competition. The RICHARD PECK, the CITY OF LOWELL, and the PRISCILLA were being built by the contending Sound services. The ambitious New Haven, irked by its lack of a direct rail entry into Boston, was eying the prosperous and extremely popular Old Colony Railroad. Two rail accidents, an eagerly sought forty-four mile stretch of valuable trackage, coupled with the allure of water travel on Long Island Sound, all were factors leading to the launching of the nautical royalty of 1907-08.

After shaking the chaff out of the complex New England transportation story of the eighties and nineties, here are the solid kernels. On March 4, 1887, a Boston and Providence Railroad local fell through a bridge near the Forest Hills station. Many historians feel that the B & P's lease to the Old Colony Railroad a year later was influenced by this disastrous accident. The B & P had been swamped with claims to the tune of a million dollars. Other authorities insist that the Old Colony leased the Boston and Providence to block the entry of the

[4] YALE and PRISCILLA were selected by Frank O. Braynard in *Famous American Ships*.

Morgan-financed New Haven into Boston. Under the lease terms, a million in cash went to the Boston and Providence, together with a guarantee of fixed charges and ten per cent yearly on its stock.

Two years later another train wreck played a role in an even more important lease. The Old Colony's Cape Cod express was derailed near Quincy, causing twenty-three deaths and many serious injuries. Now it was the Old Colony which was beset with staggering claims. There are many who hold that this 1890 accident was the prime factor in the Old Colony's deal with the New Haven. However, A. Archibald McLeod, president of the Philadelphia and Reading, was not just a bit actor in the drama. He desired a monopoly of the anthracite coal traffic and "invaded New England,"[5] a territory sacred to Pierpont Morgan. McLeod obtained an interest in the Boston and Maine Railroad and the control of the New York and New England, a spirited competitor of the New Haven. McLeod let it be known that the Old Colony and its steamboats would be a distinct addition to his budding empire. Morgan was wrathful; his hostility toward the "wild man McLeod" became common knowledge.

The New Haven simply had to have that forty-four mile Boston and Providence Railroad! But the coveted B & P was leased to the Old Colony. All right then, there was nothing to do but grab off the Old Colony, rolling stock, terminals, and steamboats. Morgan vowed that the poacher McLeod was not going to get it. Out of the blue, there was a sudden and vigorous Stock Exchange attack on the shares of the Reading as well as on the New York and New England. In a few days the Reading road was in receivership and McLeod on the way out! Meanwhile, astute brokers were quietly gathering Old Colony stock. In 1893 the New Haven leased the whole Old Colony system.[6] Actually, the New Haven only needed the

[5] Via Poughkeepsie Bridge over the Hudson.

[6] June 1958 the New Haven abandoned all passenger service on the Old Colony. It was resumed when the State granted a subsidy.

forty-four miles from Providence to Boston to insure the long-desired single-system Shore Line. In addition to the Providence-Boston link, the New Haven got 600 miles of busy track and the Old Colony's world-famed Fall River Line, which almost controlled the travel by Long Island Sound. The New Bedford Line of steamers, an immense freight carrier, was also part of the package. The Old Colony was reputed to be one of the gilt-edged railroad properties of the nation. All true Yankees loved it.

Principally through the leasing of smaller railroads which owned steamboats, the expanding New Haven Railroad had acquired a whole family of Long Island Sound steamer lines by 1900. The railroad controlled the Fall River Line, the Providence Line, the Norwich Line, the Stonington Line, and the New Bedford Line. The Bridgeport and New Haven services were also being absorbed.

Captain Jacob W. Miller, steamer executive, wrote these prophetic words to the new railroad management: "A broad comprehension of the commerce of the future shows the necessity of steamboat lines controlled by railroad interests. Such steamboat lines will always exist; as independent companies they may harass the railroads and disturb rates . . . Long Island Sound stretches for one hundred miles eastward of New York, *being a multiple track road paralleling the New Haven system. The right of way is open to all; competition is free. There will always be steamers on the Sound and it is manifest that the railroads should control them.*" A further statement by Miller proves that he was indeed farsighted. "In order to hold the large freight business from the eastern mills we should eventually have a truck service to deliver the freight direct to the New York stores" was his forecast.[7]

As Captain Miller had predicted, the increasingly ambitious New Haven Railroad soon found to its sorrow that Long

[7] New England Transportation Company, bus and truck service, was formed by the New Haven in 1925.

Island Sound, "the parallel multiple track road" was open to all; that "competition was free"—and frequent! The five years prior to Morse's daring announcement that he would inaugurate fifteen-hour deluxe steamer service direct to Boston were as wild and weird as will be found anywhere in transportation history. We can only touch on them briefly. New York to New England steamer lines sprang up; the railroad, now owning steamboats galore, created "cheap lines" of its own to fight the competitors off. Failing that, the railroad bought the intruders out at fancy prices.

In 1899 a so-called Manhattan Steamship Company attempted to buck the railroad, the Metropolitan Line (freight), and the Maine Steamship Company for Boston and "down East" business. They ended up with "less than $1000 in assets and twenty-two cents in the bank." However, that failure did not deter other steamboaters. Frank M. Dunbaugh, Allen Joy, and C. L. Dimon started the Joy Steamship Company, a freight service between New York and Providence, and a combination freight and passenger service, New York and Boston, using the paddler OLD DOMINION, a New York-Norfolk veteran. Chester W. Chapin, Jr., came on the New York-Providence run with the Narragansett Bay Line.[8]

Chapin, whose father had engaged in Connecticut steamboating, secretly leased dock property in Providence, commissioned A. Cary Smith to design a new, fast twin-screw passenger steamer and early in 1899 announced the establishment of the Narragansett Bay Line, Providence and New York, making stops at New Haven. His steamers were the RICHARD PECK and the SHINNECOCK, chartered to make a few trips while the sidewheeler C. H. NORTHAM completed an overhaul. A. Cary Smith's new CHESTER W. CHAPIN came from her builders in a few weeks. The New York-Providence passenger fare of $2.50 ($4.00 round trip), presaged a rate war. It was the first deviation in Providence steamboat fare since 1877.

[8] *The Old Fall River Line,* op. cit., p. 95.

Pierpont Morgan had frequently used his lavish yacht CORSAIR as the conference room for the consummation of some of his biggest financial deals. When, after a few months of white-hot competition, the New Haven road decided that Chapin's New York-Providence via New Haven steamers were far too troublesome to be further tolerated, a launch from the CORSAIR brought a humble Morgan aboard Chapin's schooner yacht IROQUOIS for negotiation. The circumstances plainly indicate that the railroad had been "worried into purchasing the Narragansett Bay Line." Marine men rejoiced that the "munificent price paid will enable Chapin to spend the summer in Europe untrammeled by steamboat cares." Narragansett Bay Line service terminated in April 1900. *Marine Journal,* in an editorial said, "When a steamboat company gets the better of a powerful railroad we feel like climbing to the roof and exulting in shouts loud and long." Years later in a federal trial against the monopolistic New Haven, Chapin threw the government lawyers for a decided loss by testifying that in the Central New England Railway and Narragansett Bay Line deals he had "fought the New Haven at a profit to himself."

The Joy Steamship Company was not quite so fortunate in its conflict with the railroad. Certainly they brought no joy to the New Haven. For several years they operated competitive service New York and Boston direct; New York and Providence; New York and Fall River.

When Chapin's New York-Providence service ceased, the *Marine Journal* deplored the fact that travelers were at "the mercy of a railroad corporation." The magazine suggested there might be a profitable field for the Metropolitan or Joy freight lines to develop an all-water passenger route between New York and Boston in competition with the railroad's Fall River and Providence lines. That bold suggestion was tempered with the warning, "this will not appeal to passengers liable to be seasick." In mid-May 1900 the publication was gratified to announce that the Joy's OLD DOMINION would begin carrying passengers New York to Boston direct, leaving Pier 35, East

River, New York, every Wednesday and Saturday night at five o'clock. With good luck the voyage would consume twenty-four hours, four times as long as by train.

In 1900 the idea of sailing all the way to Boston was so revolutionary that a marine publication devoted a whole column to an enlightening conversation between two travelers:

"Did you ever go to Boston by steamer?" asked the worldly-wise voyager.

"Why certainly, many times on the Fall River Line."

"No, no—that isn't going to Boston—you have to take a train part way."

"Well, there are freight boats[9] that go outside, but who wants to go that way?"

"That's where you are wrong, my friend—there is a first-class steamer to Boston. The route has a happy name, too—Joy Line. Captain Durkee can preside at the table as gracefully as the master of the biggest liner; besides he knows every inch of the way."

The Joy Line fare direct to Boston was $3.00. Reading the marine columns from 1900 on indicates that the Joy Line (also operating between New York and Providence) did a consistently flourishing business. As late as 1905 *Nautical Gazette* reported, "The Joy Line's twenty-four to thirty-hour steamer to Boston is often at a loss to know where to stow passengers, so numerous are the applications." A second steamer was necessary to run opposite the OLD DOMINION. Among the ships which served were the SEABOARD; the SURPRISE (well named, since she was the ex-CITY OF FITCHBURG of the New Bedford Line); the COCOA, from the Peninsular and Occidental Line; the Morgan Line's ARANSAS, and the SANTIAGO from the Ward Line. The popularity of Joy's Boston service, despite delays at Hell Gate, slow passages, and frequent accidents, was not exceedingly joyful to Mellen and his railroad cohorts. Probably

[9] Metropolitan Line freighters carried a few passengers.

officials of the embattled railroad did not dare use the word "joy" except with a snort!

When, in July 1900, two months after Chapin's opposition had been liquidated for a price, the Joy Line began all year round passenger service, Providence and New York, the railroad decided on different tactics. They were not going to pay through the nose twice! Joy's one-way passenger tariff was a dollar. Soon, the New Line appeared (railroad-sponsored) advertising luxurious overnight service at *fifty cents!* The railroad's big sidewheeler MASSACHUSETTS sailed alternate nights out of each port. In the height of the summer the "cheap line" (the New Haven winced at the derogatory designation) was carrying 800 or more passengers every trip. The railroad's customary summer Providence Line transported the nabobs at $3.00 a head. But the Joy Line continued doing a thriving business. Its early steamers included the ROSALIE, the CITY OF RICHMOND, the SHINNECOCK and the TREMONT. Later the CUMBERLAND and the STATE OF MAINE were secured and renamed LARCHMONT and EDGEMONT.

Because the Joy Line reported an "immense business," both passenger and freight even during the winter, the railroad really put the "new" into their New Line. The swank liners CHESTER W. CHAPIN, CITY OF LOWELL and even the Fall River liner PLYMOUTH were put on the low-fare Providence run. As summer neared, the big luxury ships were needed for more revenue-producing services and the sidewheelers RHODE ISLAND and CONNECTICUT were refurbished and became the poor man's friend. The *Providence Journal of Commerce* waxed indignant at the railroad's heartless New Line tactics. "The daily service on its 'cheap line' is for no other purpose than to injure the Joy Steamship Company. It is an act which should have been beneath such a wealthy and prosperous organization as the New Haven Road. If the railroad desired to give the public, who could not afford passage on its *high-price boats,* an opportunity to travel, it could have favored them long before the Joy Line was in existence. It could have also, before the past season, given Providence a passenger service during the winter."

The competition for Providence business was fierce and relentless until the autumn of 1902. A "harmonious agreement" as to rates was worked out and the railroad withdrew its New Line on October 31. In an editorial the *Providence Evening Telegram* stated the conviction of many traffic experts; neither company had gained an advantage. "It is true that the boats were jammed to capacity every trip" declared the paper, "but that did not mean much profit. While the railroad's 'cheap line' carried capacity loads, their three dollar boat, on an average, had only about enough to fill the pilot house. The wear and tear has been appalling. Every steamer put on by the railroad was nearly ruined by the class of passengers."

In the meantime Joy's OLD DOMINION plodded to and fro between New York and Boston. She had very little power[10] and found roaring Hell Gate troublesome. Often, when she met a head tide at Hell Gate she was stymied. Tugs huffed and puffed her through or she anchored for hours in New York's East River.

Travelers who remember the OLD DOMINION on the Boston run have widely divergent views concerning the quality of her service. William B. Taylor, of Milton, Massachusetts, recalls an October 1905 round-trip voyage from Boston as "most pleasant." On the return, the OLD DOMINION left New York late at night with a good passenger list, according to Taylor's recollection. When he arose early the next morning and glanced at the shoreline, the Boston-bound Taylor probably ejaculated, "The hell you say!" But let Taylor unfold the saga of what appears to have been a typical voyage. "The OLD DOMINION only made ten knots so we didn't get out of the East River very lively. With the coming of morning everything seemed unusually quiet. I was surprised when I went on deck

[10] On the Old Dominion Line she had once been known for speed.

to find we were anchored close to Hell Gate. The ship had hand steering and it was deemed unsafe to navigate Hell Gate against a head tide. When the tide changed we proceeded. That gave us all day on the Sound in daylight and it was delightful sailing. We came over Nantucket Shoals about sunset."

My esteemed friend John J. DeMott, now of North Carolina, recalls the OLD DOMINION, Boston to New York, rather unpleasantly. He and a brother sat the night out in a small deckhouse smoking room because their stateroom was populated by a host of "bloodsucking hemipterous insects." "The next day," said DeMott, "most of the passengers were too tired to enjoy very much." On this trip the OLD DOMINION went outside of Long Island rather than through the Sound and consequently Hell Gate was no obstacle. To DeMott, an experienced world traveler, the OLD DOMINION "was more suggestive of pre-Civil War days than any boat I ever traveled on." (She was built in 1872.)

Boyhood memories of the OLD DOMINION still captivate Burtis D. Miles, of New Rochelle, New York. He and another lad were given a Joy Line New York to Boston pass by the nephew of C. L. Dimon, one of the Joy triumvirate. The two sat in the mysterious darkness of the circular pilot house nearly all night and had a sumptuous meal with the captain at 2 A.M. "We boys stuffed ourselves and weren't seasick" is his prideful boast. Miles's father did not caper for joy at his son's Joy Line adventure and begged him to stay home because, "Joy Line boats are always getting into trouble."

The record bears out the senior Miles's contention. In their short span on Long Island Sound, Joy Line ships were involved in mishaps aplenty. Loss of the LARCHMONT in February 1907 was one of the nation's appalling marine disasters. The TREMONT, with 350 passengers, nearly foundered in July 1900, after a collision with the iron yacht WILD DUCK. Captain William B. Appleby, later one of COMMONWEALTH'S most famous skippers, then in command of Stonington's NEW

HAMPSHIRE, beached the stricken Joy liner in New London. That autumn the OLD DOMINION was layed up for several weeks when she struck a schooner in the Sound. The year 1901 was marked by a serious accident which almost put the OLD DOMINION out of commission. In fog, she ploughed ashore at Rye Beach, New York, and could not be floated off for weeks. Two years later, the OLD DOMINION was badly damaged in an encounter with a schooner off Cape Cod. Later her running mate, the SEABOARD, went aground at Boston during a dense fog. In February 1904, the TREMONT was totally destroyed by fire at her New York pier, giving rise to the Sound's famous lion story.[11] In May 1905, the ARANSAS was sunk near Pollock Rip in collision with a coal barge. The year closed with a serious fire on the ROSALIE.

The old adage that "there is always room for one more" was proved late in 1904. A rumor that "Fall River parties" had bought the 161-foot-long iron vessel CONOBO, built in 1881, and would operate her, Fall River to New York, was the forerunner of highly disturbing news to the New Haven. The railroad was having troubles enough with the Joy Line's two competing services and the certainty of Morse's future rivalry, without facing steamboat conflict nearer home. Captain Jacob W. Miller, general manager of the railroad's marine properties, was known as a seer of the highest rank. You will remember his prediction when the New Haven bought and consolidated steamboat services, that "Long Island Sound is a right of way open to all; independent companies may harass the railroad and disturb rates."

The Fall River Line's new passenger ship PROVIDENCE had her coming-out party in June 1905. The glory of that event was tarnished for the New Haven by the announcement that the Enterprise Transportation Company, headed by David Whitcomb, of Worcester, would begin freight and passenger service Fall River and New York. An independent steamer line

[11] *The Old Fall River Line,* op. cit., p. 178.

out of Fall River! What next! The Enterprise steamers, scheduled to stop at Jamestown, Rhode Island, opposite Newport, were the FRANK JONES, from Maine waters, and the WARREN. The propeller WARREN was an old friend come back to plague those who had cast her adrift. She was the ex-CITY OF FITCHBURG; ex-SURPRISE. The FRANK JONES was described by the *Rockland Courier-Gazette* as "the handsomest and only really modern sidewheeler north of Cape Cod." Built in 1892, the FRANK JONES had the reputation of being a bad roller and had a thunderous whistle, the vibrations of which, it was claimed, "cracked window panes." News accounts touted the FRANK JONES for "beautiful appointments including steam heat and electric lights." [12]

To the consternation of the beleaguered New Haven Railroad, the Enterprise service (often called the New Line) caught on. It was a boon to the thrifty. Plunking a dollar down at the ticket window assured a through passage between New York and Fall River. Twenty cents more supplied a ticket between New York and Providence via Fall River. The through fare New York and Boston was $2.20. After a brief two months of Enterprise operation, *Nautical Gazette* trumpeted, "The Enterprise Line between New York and Fall River, a route made famous by the Old Colony service, has leaped into immediate popularity.[13] The venture seems to have justified the expectation of the founder. The FRANK JONES, although far from offering the extensive accommodations of the PRISCILLA and PURITAN, is a modern, well-appointed steamer." In another month the Enterprise folk bought the popular sidewheeler KENNEBEC from the Eastern Steamship Company. The KENNEBEC, while plying between Boston and Bath for more than twenty years, was affectionately known as the "old home ship." To add

[12] *Steamboat Lore of the Penobscot,* John M. Richardson, Augusta, Maine, 1946, p. 67.

[13] July 26, the FRANK JONES was forced to leave freight and passengers at New York. Brought record cargo and 324 passengers to Fall River.

to the indignity, Enterprise added a Providence to New York service with steamers St. Croix and Warren. Never had the Sound been so crowded, the wharves so busy and the New Haven so agitated!

Shippers and travelers were chortling. For a change the breaks of the game favored them. Freight rates and passenger tariffs were sharply reduced. The war between the steamship companies dropped the cost of transporting a barrel of sugar, Fall River to New York, to the paltry sum of five cents a barrel; a barrel of oil could be shipped over the waterway for eight cents. The conventional Fall River Line newspaper display advertisements showed the full effect of the Enterprise and Joy lines competition. Mere sailing schedules suddenly became persuasive and intensive sales messages. A Fall River Line advertisement published in New York in December 1905 emphasized "lowest rates; unsurpassed steamers Providence (new) and Plymouth; *perfect* connecting train service at Fall River; orchestra on each steamer; baggage checked through; staterooms for two persons $1.00 and $2.00; first class berths free." The Fall River Line fares shown in the advertisement were New York to Boston $2.00;[14] New York to Newport, Fall River, and Providence $1.50. (From this it would appear that the railroad absorbed the cost of transporting passengers from Fall River Wharf to Providence, potent evidence of their desire to scuttle the Joy Line, New York and Providence.) Passengers flocked to all piers; the Enterprise Line frequently had to put the spare boat Warren on to handle the big cotton shipments.

The year 1906 was a period of rumor and hard fact for the railroad. Except the post-Civil War era, when Jim Fisk's Bristol Line battled the Stonington and Fall River lines and the fares dropped to fifty cents, no other twelve-month competitive period was comparable. In June, the Enterprise revealed that it had plans ready for the construction of four new

[14] Enterprise Line fare New York to Boston was $1.75.

steamers, two of them turbine-driven. On July 11, the Joy Line entered the Fall River field. Their passenger steamers were the TENNESSEE, from Chesapeake's Old Bay Line, and the KENTUCKY, which was the ex-LINCOLN, ex-MARTINIQUE. In September, an unfounded rumor had Morse as the purchaser of the Enterprise Line. In November, the Fall River Line made the unprecedented announcement that the big summer liners PRISCILLA and PURITAN would continue in winter service.

Everybody and his uncle was voyaging Long Island Sound in 1906, if the Fall River Line passenger traffic is an indication. Staterooms and the free dormitory berths were at a premium nightly; hundreds of eager travelers slept on mattresses spread in the luxurious lounge rooms. In the face of the Joy Line's two-pronged competition and the rival Enterprise service at its home port, the Fall River Line carried more passengers in 1906 than in any other year. The total was 444,500, nearly 100,000 more than were transported in 1905 when the fury of rate-cutting really began. In only one other year, before or after, did the Line transport more than 400,000. The PRISCILLA's second season, 1895, had established the previous high, 426,975.

Mellen was not twiddling his thumbs in New Haven while these new companies were challenging the railroad's control of the New England seaway. His friendly trolley lines cut connections with the Enterprise Line steamers. The Pennsylvania Railroad declined to participate with the Enterprise in through freight rates to Philadelphia. The railroad's maligned "cheap line" had forced the Joy Line to stabilize passenger fares in 1902. Those tactics might work again. In October 1905, Mellen let the railroad directors know how simple it would be to rid the Sound of interlopers. "We should establish a *seemingly independent line* to build up our low class steamship passenger business" he dictated to his secretary. "There seems to be a marked demand for such a service. *Once we secure control of the low-class service,* we should acquire the Hartford and New York Transportation Company."

Early in 1907, the great game of kidding the public began with the sly announcement that another "competitor" to the railroad's Fall River Line would enter the already overcrowded territory. The new United States Transportation Company was made known. The "seemingly independent" service "bought" the idle sidewheelers CONNECTICUT and RHODE ISLAND from the railroad, of all people. Despite this transaction, Mellen waxed indignant at the suggestion "the United States Transportation Company is considered in marine circles to be a New Haven Railroad Company." When the new outfit's list of officers was revealed, even the gullible public guffawed at Mellen's sharp denials of the railroad's financial interest in the venture. Stevenson Taylor was the president of the United States Transportation Company; George Q. Palmer, secretary-treasurer, and Warren T. Berry, superintending engineer. In their spare time Taylor and Berry were designing the railroad's new COMMONWEALTH; Palmer was an officer of Quintard Iron Works,[15] beneficiary of the contracts for the building of BUNKER HILL, COMMONWEALTH, MASSACHUSETTS and OLD COLONY. In May 1907, the United States Transportation's Neptune Line provided a fourth overnight steamer between Fall River and New York! A dollar bought a Neptune Fall River-New York ticket; two dollars covered a passage between New York and Boston. Neptune tried to convince the public that they were providing service of Fall River Line standards. Did not the Neptune's CONNECTICUT and RHODE ISLAND have "commodious staterooms and home comforts; orchestra on each steamer; superior cuisine; all modern safety appliances including wireless"? Were not their "train and trolley connections convenient and frequent"? Was not their wharf at Baylies Street "only two minutes walk from the Fall River Railroad Station"? Neptune's folder summed up their attributes with the bland statement

[15] Quintard had built U.S.S. MAINE, blown up in Havana, a cause of the Spanish-American War.

that they were "the family route between New York and New England." All of this for a dollar, mind you!

The unconvincing "seemingly independent" pitch for the Neptune Line did not last very long. To begin with, there was a rumor that the PURITAN and the PLYMOUTH would come off the aristocratic run to replace the Neptune's sidewheelers. Another tip-off on the "enmity" of the two lines was the fact that some Fall River Line personnel manned Neptune steamers. It is interesting to observe that Captain Frank H. Avery commanded Neptune's RHODE ISLAND. Thirty years later, the same Avery handled the COMMONWEALTH on her final voyage, New York to Fall River.

The real warfare was between the cheap and elite rail-owned lines on one hand and the "blackmail" Enterprise and Joy steamers on the other. And it was war-bitter, constant, destructive, and relentless! The Fall River waterfront was the liveliest place in town when the late afternoon Boston trains and trolleys arrived. (Regular Fall River Line travelers were taken direct to the steamer by the boat train. Consequently, they were not subjected to hawking and brawling.) The Neptune Line (Baylies Street) and Enterprise Line (Turner Street) docks were close to each other; Central Street, from which the Joy Line sailed, was nearer Fall River Wharf. Passengers heading for the waterfront were besieged by negro porters from the various lines. Valises were almost torn apart as dark hands representing Enterprise, Joy, and Neptune lines reached for them. Fist fights and bloody noses often resulted. It is amazing how much confusion existed on Davol Street, paralleling the harbor. Porters must have been both blind and deaf. Ticket holders for the Enterprise Line frequently found themselves on the Neptune or Joy steamers or vice versa. Many voyagers were unaware of the error until halfway down Mount Hope Bay. It is said that family groups at times got separated in the bewilderment of smiling porters and noisy barkers. They tearfully waved at each other as the rival steamers passed. The only comforting thought was that both vessels were headed for New York.

The railroad's squeeze play worked. The Joy Line's Fall River-New York service was short-lived. The Enterprise Transportation Company went into receivership in November 1907. The Neptune Line, like the railroad's earlier "cheap line" (New Line between New York and Providence), disappeared in February 1908. Once again the historic Fall River Line was unfettered except for Morse's projected direct Boston service, for which steamers YALE and HARVARD were being constructed.

Within days of each other two events early in February 1907 shuffled the cards. Positive statements appeared in leading newspapers that Morse had bought the Fall River Line and other marine properties of the New Haven Railroad, including the uncompleted fast freighters BUNKER HILL, MASSACHUSETTS and OLD COLONY. The purchase price was a cool twenty million. On the night of February 11, the Joy liner LARCHMONT was sunk off Watch Hill with an appalling loss of life. On February 14 it was officially announced that the New Haven had rejected Morse's bid. Mellen admitted that Morse had made "a very liberal offer and was refused, not for lack of appreciation of it, but because it is against the policy of the New Haven to part with any of its property." Days before, the New Haven had acquired the Maine Steamship Company—that is, "Stevenson Taylor and associates" had signed the purchase contract. And Morse had added the New York-Cuba Ward Line to his growing steamship holdings. Financiers and marine men knew that the New Haven's "nothing doing" answer to Morse meant there would be something doing on Long Island Sound!

Ten musicians placed their personal baggage and instruments aboard the Joy Line steamer LARCHMONT, at Providence, New York bound, on the evening of February 11, 1907. They were off to Baltimore to fill a short vaudeville theater engagement. A forty-mile wind howled and the temperature hovered close to the zero mark. The tuba player, Ricardo Riccardi, and his companions entered a barroom off South Main Street to warm themselves for the expected cold and rough voyage to New York. In the hour of conviviality the warning whistles of the LARCHMONT fell on deaf ears. When the merry musicians staggered to the dock, they found it cheerless and empty. Their baggage, their musical paraphernalia and the LARCHMONT were gone. How literally they knew not!

Half frozen, but carefree and light-hearted, they stumbled the several blocks to the railroad station and took a train for New York. The next morning they made their way to the Joy Line's East River pier to pick up their belongings. There was an air of excitement and tension as they crossed South Street to the wharf. Many were milling about a crudely printed sign bearing the ominous news—"The LARCHMONT was sunk during the night."

While the happy-go-lucky musicians, amused at being on a train instead of a steamboat, chugged toward New York, a cub reporter in Fall River, assigned to the newsy "four New York boats a night" waterfront, retired about midnight. It was bitterly cold but there was a brilliant moon and many stars were out. Before dawn there was a persistent tapping on the reporter's bedroom door.

"You're wanted on the phone."

Sleepily muttering into the telephone the reporter heard a familiar voice, "This is Hal Edson at the Joy Line office. You better come right down." Edson declined to give a hint of the reason for the urgent early morning "come right down."

After dressing hurriedly, the reporter braved the icy winds and headed for the Joy Line office at the foot of Central Street. Solemn faces greeted the newsman. "The LARCHMONT, out of Providence, has been sunk in Block Island Sound with a great loss of life," the chief clerk said. "We're getting up steam on the KENTUCKY to go down to Block Island from here." Details of the catastrophe were meager because of absence of wireless on Joy Line steamers and limited phone service.

On the morning of February 12, Mrs. Riccardi answered her North Providence doorbell. After the postman's customary greetings he said, "It's terrible about the sinking of the LARCHMONT, isn't it?" Mrs. Riccardi almost fainted. "The LARCHMONT sunk—my husband was on that ship last night!" The postman was greatly disturbed that he had unwittingly been the bearer of sad news. Later the grief-stricken wife was taken to a morgue in an attempt to have her identify her husband's body.

Riccardi and his fellow musicians left the confusion and distress at New York's Joy Line pier and continued on to Baltimore. Hours elapsed before he sent a telegram to his wife telling of his safe arrival. For some unaccountable reason the telegram created doubt among officials. They were certain Riccardi had perished on the LARCHMONT. Repeatedly Mrs. Riccardi was brought to the Providence morgue to examine unclaimed bodies. When letters started arriving from Riccardi, the authorities decided that maybe he was alive after all.

The harrowing tales and the heroism associated with the loss of the ill-fated wooden LARCHMONT,[16] in collision with the schooner HARRY KNOWLTON, loaded with 500 tons of coal, are told in the author's *Salts of the Sound*. There were only nineteen survivors. Bodies encased in ice washed up on the bleak Block Island shore for days. Early estimates of the dead and missing stood at 189; the official count of the lost was ultimately recorded as 131. The Rhode Island General Assembly referred to the tragic night as "a calamity unparalleled in the history of the navigation of local waters."

When the LARCHMONT went down, really finishing the Joy Line as a transportation entity, three of the six "1907 nautical royalty" had already been launched. The disaster brought home to the ship designers the value of steel double hulls and

[16] In 1902 the LARCHMONT, then named CUMBERLAND, had been sunk in Boston harbor.

watertight compartments. It convinced operating officials of the necessity for wireless, in use on the Fall River Line for about three years, as the means of summoning aid instantly.

First of the nautical royalty to be launched was the YALE, which caused a big splash late in 1906. The next few months saw a frenzy of launchings, trial trips, claims and counterclaims, speed records made and broken, climaxed by hot disagreements as to the merits of turbine or sidewheel propulsion.

The names selected by Morse for his new liners were not so much a tribute to famous Yankee institutions of learning as a recognition of the fact that one son of the Maine steamship tycoon was a student at Yale while another was at Harvard. On Saturday, December 1, the Connecticut university took possession of Roach's Chester, Pennsylvania, shipyard. As Yale flags whipped in the breeze, Laura B. Hadley, eight-year-old daughter of university President Arthur T. Hadley, in the presence of thousands of cheering spectators, gave the ship, festooned with blue bunting, her name. The gala day for Yale University also marked another victory for Morse. He had enticed the popular Orlando H. Taylor, general passenger agent of the Fall River Line, to become head of the Metropolitan Line's passenger traffic. Taylor's many lavish Fall River Line launching parties had become famous; he spared nothing to make the YALE festivities an extraordinary success. A twelve-car Pullman train brought the Morse family and distinguished guests to Chester. In a few days, the YALE was towed to the Hoboken plant of W. & A. Fletcher Company for final construction, and the Roach yard prepared to float the HARVARD.

Morse had no monopoly of the marine columns early in February 1907. His HARVARD, third turbine ship to be built in the United States, was launched on January 29. At the same time the nearby Cramp yard matched the event by putting Mellen's freighter MASSACHUSETTS into the water. Ruth Eliot, sixteen-year-old granddaughter of Harvard's illustrious president, christened the passenger craft. The celebration was witnessed by several thousand guests, who were "the recipients of openhearted hospitality ministered by Traffic Manager Taylor." John B. Roach modestly admitted that "no finer launch ever took place." Taylor's genius was evident in the publicity releases. The HARVARD was described as "revolutionary in mechanical details but with furnishings on a scale so elaborate *as to make them noteworthy for all time.*" Stress was laid on her forty parlor suites with hot and cold running water.[17] The "important launch" of the MASSACHUSETTS, first of the railroad's three freighters for the all-water route, was "a success in every way." She was christened by Mrs. George Quintard Palmer, wife of Quintard Iron Works' general manager. Two months later (March 28) BUNKER HILL, christened by Miss Rose Elizabeth Fitzgerald, daughter of Boston's mayor, left the Cramp ways.

Gardner, Taylor, and Haas faced peculiar problems in conceiving the three freighters. While intended for the outside route, it was stipulated they must be able to operate with equal facility to the intermediate ports of New Haven, New London, Providence, or Fall River. Limited passenger accommodations were to be provided. BUNKER HILL, MASSACHUSETTS and OLD COLONY were absolutely alike as to model and boiler power. However, OLD COLONY had a direct-drive Parsons turbine triple screw installation; the other two had twin four-cylinder triple-expansion reciprocating engines. The trio were unique in that the boilers were located in two separate compartments, four boilers in each. The heavy steel hulls were divided into ten watertight compartments by nine bulkheads, having no doors or openings, extending from the keel to the uppermost structural deck.

As the technicians at Newport Shops wrestled with the complexities, Gardner made an unusual proposal. Calling a conference he said, "We here in Newport are specialists in

[17] When built, HARVARD and YALE had "more bathrooms than any other coastwise ships."

building big sidewheelers but our experience in designing fast propeller ships has been a bit limited. I suggest that we have Cramps also prepare a model. The two models are to have precisely the same displacement, draft, and general dimensions. Then we will have both tested in the Naval Tank and weigh the results. Remember, gentlemen, that our steamers must match the speed of the Morse ships." The plan was carried out and Newport was elated at the news from Admiral David W. Taylor. Experiments showed that at the designed power the Newport Shop's model beat the Cramp model by one-half knot!

Construction of the new ships was rushed. Mellen and Gardner scored first with the speed claims. The MASSACHUSETTS left Cramps on May 25. On June 4, with eight hundred tons of freight for Fall River, she left Pier 18 North River, New York, at 3:12 P.M. She arrived at Fall River Wharf 7 hours, 48 minutes later, averaging twenty knots for the entire distance. Immediately, *Nautical Gazette* hailed the new craft as "the speediest vessel ever built for Long Island Sound." Aboard the MASSACHUSETTS on her first service trip were Gardner, Taylor, Berry, and Captains Miller and Henry O. Nickerson, who were unanimous in expressing "unbounded enthusiasm for the new ship." The MASSACHUSETTS that night smashed the mark set by the old METROPOLIS back in June 1855. Conflicting times have been recorded for the METROPOLIS's New York-Fall River record. The best mark is given as 8 hours, 21 minutes; other old records for the same voyage show it as 8 hours, 51 minutes. (When the PRISCILLA raced the CITY OF LOWELL, July 21, 1894, she made the 95-statute-mile stretch, Throggs' Neck to Little Gull Island, in 4 hours, 32 minutes. On her first trip the MASSACHUSETTS covered the same distance in 4 hours, 2 minutes, 34 seconds.)

The OLD COLONY was launched by Cramps on June 26. In October the sidewheeler COMMONWEALTH became the last of the noble sextette to be floated upon the waters of the Delaware River. Three days after the OLD COLONY left the ways, the completed YALE took special guests from New York to

Boston. Immediately the speed of the MASSACHUSETTS was forgotten. The YALE, with seething water boiling astern, zoomed into Boston in less than 14 hours, despite necessary slowing down in the East River and a tide against her at both Hell Gate and The Race. Her incredible average for the entire distance was 21.45 knots! The statisticians computed that adverse tides had cut at least one knot from her average.

It was Morse's day. The *Nautical Gazette,* enraptured by the swift but steady voyage of the YALE, did not hesitate to hint that the New Haven had cause to worry. "The remarkable performance of the YALE will astonish the patrons of the regular Long Island Sound railroad-steamboat lines," it bluntly stated. "While steaming at the highest speed, the YALE's vibration at the stern was barely perceptible. Forward or amidships the craft might still have been on the stocks for all the motion that was felt. As evidence of the quiet running of the ship, the large sideboard at the after end of the main deck dining room was filled with glassware. There was not the slightest vibration or tinkle to be heard."

The YALE's luxurious accommodations were not neglected in the paean. "No American steamer yet built has so elaborate and beautiful a scheme of embellishment. Yale blue is the color wherever practical, such as carpeting and upholstery. The dining room is one of the largest, airiest, and most beautiful to be found on any vessel, ocean-going or inland."

A week later the marine reporters were searching for new descriptives to describe the speed shown on Long Island Sound. The railroad's freighter BUNKER HILL left the builders at Philadelphia on July 8. Coming up the coast to New York she averaged 20.44 knots. She joined the MASSACHUSETTS in freight service, New York and Fall River. There were gasps of sheer unbelief when nautical men heard that BUNKER HILL dashed from Execution Rocks to Point Judith (122½ statute miles) in the amazing time of 4 hours, 58 minutes.

For all the favorable publicity and heavy cargoes, the big black rockets brought some woe to the New Haven. Truckers at Fall River demanded an increase in wages from 17½ cents to 20 cents an hour because the new speedsters necessitated their arrival at the pier at 4 A.M. Then the longshoremen sent up a plea for a "second shift" due to the early arrival of the express freighters. Late in October they refused to report for work at the ungodly hour. Their places were filled by newly arrived immigrants, and a lockout ensued.

Because the HARVARD was not ready, the YALE was employed during the summer on the Boston-St. John, New Brunswick, route. By mid-September both of Morse's flyers were available to begin the New York-Boston passenger service. Mellen retaliated with the threat that his fast freighters would be hauled off the New York-Fall River run to open an opposition Boston freight line round the Cape. No jeers came from the dock workers at Fall River Wharf!

Did the BUNKER HILL beat the HARVARD? If so, was it "many times" or just one night when the "HARVARD had engine trouble?" Veteran shipmasters testify both ways. Fall River Line mariners Captains Norman L. Strickland and Frank H. Bunce, who served on the railroad's "outside line" (Boston Merchants Line) insist that the BUNKER HILL left the HARVARD astern frequently. Metropolitan Line skippers scoff at such reckless assertions. Captain Harold L. Colbeth, of the HARVARD, and later of the MASSACHUSETTS when she became a passenger liner, scores claims of the BUNKER HILL partisans with surprising vehemence.

The only concession from Colbeth was "HARVARD had engine trouble—*once.*" Possibly October 4, 1907, was the night of the mechanical difficulty. Unless the pilot houses were filled with perjurers or the newspapers lied, one of the Sound's most exciting matches unexpectedly was staged that autumn night. Newspapers and marine publications devoted considerable space to the encounter. BUNKER HILL bested HARVARD; the author has discovered no denials of the fact from Morse minions. Freeman R. Hathaway, past president of *The Steamship Historical Society*, writing in the June 1943 *Steamboat*

Bill, says that because of an accident sending BUNKER HILL to drydock she was "consciously or not, prepared for the race of her lifetime." On October 2, the steamer, approaching the dock in New York, sank the New Haven Railroad's tug TRANSFER No. 3. The BUNKER HILL went to the Tietjen & Lang yard in Hoboken for new twin screws. On Friday, October 4, carrying no freight, the BUNKER HILL left Hoboken at 5:23 P.M., passing Pier 18, North River, ten minutes later. After rounding Throggs' Neck, the freighter's officers discovered to their glee the Boston-bound HARVARD some six minutes ahead. Both were stepped up and the Sound fairly boiled. The BUNKER HILL, running light, had all eight boilers fired. In an hour and a half the two ran beam to beam. Finally the BUNKER HILL forged ahead. Despite two terrific spurts by the HARVARD, the BUNKER HILL held her advantage. Twelve minutes after the BUNKER HILL had rounded the Point Judith buoy and headed for Fall River, the lights of the HARVARD could be seen passing the Point. The BUNKER HILL arrived off Fall River Wharf at 12:45 A.M.—7 hours and 12 minutes after passing Pier 18, shattering the June record of the MASSACHUSETTS. In deference to her sister it must be emphasized that BUNKER HILL was carrying no cargo.

The stars of Long Island Sound—noble ships in peace and war—YALE, HARVARD, MASSACHUSETTS, BUNKER HILL, OLD COLONY, and COMMONWEALTH, are saluted here in the order of their launching!

CHAPTER THREE

"All Hands on Deck!"

In 1907 the largest and fastest ships in the world were the British-built Cunarders LUSITANIA and MAURETANIA. For their construction the British government had loaned the Cunard Line twelve and one-half million dollars. The sister ships were built to challenge the fast German liners and to counter Pierpont Morgan's new combine, the International Mercantile Marine. The British Admiralty stipulated that the giant liners be propelled by turbines with a speed of 24.5 knots in normal seas. Cunard's CARMANIA of 1905, with triple screws driven by three turbines, supplied the experimental data for the LUSITANIA and the MAURETANIA. It is said that before the 1907 giants were launched, models were subjected to five hundred tests and trials. The CARMANIA and the 1907 pair were described as representing "daring progress in the face of smashing competition."

How did the six American Sound steamers—the nautical royalty of 1907—compare with the world's largest and swiftest liners? The twin trans-Atlantic Cunarders were 790 feet long, overall, and 88 feet in extreme breadth. Fall River's COMMONWEALTH was approximately seven feet broader, could sleep almost as many passengers and carry as much freight as the LUSITANIA. The record-breaking Parsons turbine-driven LUSITANIA and MAURETANIA both consistently averaged 25 knots and cut the Atlantic crossing to four and one half days![1] The Metropolitan Line's American-built HARVARD, with Parsons direct-drive turbines, on *178 trips* navigating the congested and

[1] MAURETANIA held the Atlantic Blue Riband for twenty-two years.

frequently foggy waters between New York and Boston, averaged 20.05 knots a voyage. All six Sound steamers of 1907-08, *three of them freighters,* could maintain speeds of 20 knots. They, like the world's largest ships, represented "daring progress in the face of smashing competition."

By midsummer of 1908 all six of the new steamers were in service on the Sound. Early in the year Mellen had made good his threat. The railroad's speedy freighters BUNKER HILL and MASSACHUSETTS opened the new all-water Boston Merchants Line to foil Morse's Metropolitan Line. The Metropolitan Line, with "the costliest and most luxurious passenger steamers in America," the HARVARD and the YALE, offered travelers "the finest water trip in the world." Captain Lorenzo M. Crowell was skipper of the HARVARD. Picturesque Captain Benjamin S. Grove, who had "command of strong language," directed the YALE's nightly dashes through the Sound. That a new age was dawning was revealed in Metropolitan's advertising, which pointed out its "most satisfactory facilities for the transportation of horses *and automobiles.*" Even though many a 1908 motorist almost lost an arm attempting to crank his balky equipage to the accompaniment of cries of "get a horse," Metropolitan suggested to New Yorkers, "the charm of motor trips around historic Boston is made easily accessible by the overnight HARVARD and YALE."

On July 1, the COMMONWEALTH, "in a class apart from other craft," became the flagship of the Fall River Line. Her spacious lounges and penthouse dining room somewhat eclipsed the popularity of Morse's Boston steamers. The new COMMONWEALTH was commanded by a Stonington and Providence sidewheeler veteran, Captain George H. Williamson, who came from the PRISCILLA. Williamson, technically the "commodore" of the New Haven Railroad's fleet, approached his new command with some apprehension. After all, his inland sea passenger liner was longer by thirty feet than the new British fighting craft COMMONWEALTH, built on the Clyde five years before and designated the "world's biggest battleship."

Because of his COMMONWEALTH's bulk, Williamson foresaw difficulties lurking behind every fog bank and jagged rock at tortuous Hell Gate.

Porters and dining-room waiters on both the Fall River and Metropolitan lines found the summer of 1908 lucrative. All day long, ticket agents faced queues of hopeful voyagers. Some nights they could have sold out two or three additional steamers. Passenger officials almost dreaded answering their phones. Over and over, from personal friends or regular travelers, they heard pleas for "a good outside stateroom next Wednesday night for our firm's vice president (or my sick mother or my old college chum); the Ticket Office says you're all sold out. Can't you find something?" The heavy travel continued well beyond Labor Day.

The weather in late September 1908 had all the Sound skippers edgy. On September 18 the *New York Sun* reported that because of lusty gales "Vineyard Sound is filled with stormbound vessels." A most significant sentence in the storm dispatch was, "the passenger liner HARVARD was delayed *nearly an hour* by the gale." It was news whenever the swift HARVARD was hindered for as little as five minutes by any act of either God or man!

Mariners claim that fog in the stretch between Boston and Newport is more abundant and more impenetrable than anywhere else on the Atlantic coast. Frequency of fog was but one of the reasons the Long Island Sound-Buzzards Bay-Cape Cod route was regarded as "one of the toughest runs in the world."[2]

After the roaring winds and raging seas, nights of cottony mist plagued the mariners and jumbled timetables. On September 24 the Navy's cruiser YANKEE went hard aground at Hen and Chickens Lightship. The next evening the fog was so

[2] *Salts of the Sound,* Roger Williams McAdam: Stephen Daye Press, New York, 1957, p. 15.

thick at New York that Captain Williamson anchored the eastbound COMMONWEALTH all night in the East River. At six o'clock the next morning she threaded her way through Hell Gate. A wireless message from the COMMONWEALTH off Faulkner's Island reported her steaming through dense fog but due in Newport about 3 P.M. Annoyed rail officials arranged a special Boston train from that point. The COMMONWEALTH had her gangplank on Long Wharf at 3:07 P.M., twelve hours late. She hurriedly discharged her passengers and Newport freight and poked her way through the foamy atmosphere to Fall River.

If there ever was thicker fog in the Newport area, veterans cannot date it. Word came from treacherous Block Island that an important fog signal was out of order. The government immediately dispatched a repairman. It was three days before the worker set foot on Block Island. At Newport, seeking passage on the daily steamer NEW SHOREHAM, the lighthouse serviceman found the captain obdurate in his refusal to head out past Brenton's Reef Lightship, especially as one of Block Island's voices was silent. The NEW SHOREHAM was fogbound at Newport for two full days.

As a result of the long delay at New York, the COMMONWEALTH had to make a quick turn around at Fall River. There was feverish activity unloading and loading cargo. She took aboard for New York one of the largest passenger lists of the season. About four hours after her belated arrival she pointed her prow into the wall of whiteness, her deep-throated whistle blasting every half minute as she moved down Mount Hope Bay.

Every night aboard the massive COMMONWEALTH was soul-stirring to twenty-year-old Norman Strickland. In five short years he had been promoted from deckhand on the PURITAN to helmsman on the COMMONWEALTH. Even though he was a lowly subordinate in the pilothouse, the two-million-dollar COMMONWEALTH was partly his to control. Captain Williamson or the pilot staked their careers on the youth's strict attention to course instructions, constant check of the compass, and strong hand on the special Williamson gear steam steering wheel. It was Strickland's responsibility to keep 5980 tons, while moving at nearly twenty knots, on her true course. His nightly six-hour watch under First Pilot Senior Grade Henry Brightman was an exciting and varied apprenticeship. While every voyage was different, Strickland never forgot the drama and the terror at The Race on Saturday morning, September 26. There had been no letup in the fog. Haggard by the demands of the two-day disrupted schedule and soon to go on duty, Strickland in his bunk immediately below the pilothouse tossed fitfully between blasts of the fog whistle screaming every thirty seconds almost over his head. Between blinks and blasts he could hear the agitated questions of Captain Williamson and the low-voiced responses of First Pilot Junior Grade Daniel Grinnell, the officer on watch.

He sensed that the COMMONWEALTH had stopped and heard Grinnell say, "That whistle sounds damn close, Sir." After a minute the COMMONWEALTH started ahead under a slow bell. Suddenly there were imperative commands, COMMONWEALTH's whistle barked out the danger signal, the engine-room gong rang full speed astern, followed by a terrific impact, which almost tossed Strickland from his berth.

"Lord Almighty, she must be climbing a stone wall," cried Strickland, leaping out of bed. As he did so, the lifesaving crew's bell rang and Grinnell's voice shouted through the speaking tube, "All hands on deck! All hands on deck!"

Seconds later when Strickland reached the pilothouse Grinnell said, "Report to your boat station; we've hit another ship; it looks as if we've got her; we may be in bad shape, too." As Strickland, member of the six-man lifesaving crew, rushed to the special boat, he saw a big steamer hanging crazily on COMMONWEALTH's bow. Then she broke loose in a cloud of steam and came grinding alongside the Sound liner. Someone yelled, "Her boiler's exploded!" It was evident she was taking water fast; a woman[3] from the other ship was tossed over onto the COMMONWEALTH's deck as the two ships briefly came together. Strickland had no time to observe more because he was going down into a calm sea in the COMMONWEALTH's lifeboat. The lifesaving crew was composed of Dennis Crowley, the steamer's second mate; John Sorenson, boatswain,[4] Michael Ronan, bow watchman; Norman Strickland, quartermaster; Willian Ronan and T. Nelson, deckhands. Three other COMMONWEALTH boats also hit the water. The hissing of steam and shouts for help filled the heavy air; in the distance fog horns moaned and steamer whistles blasted. The fifteen-man crew of the other ship was rescued by the COMMONWEALTH's special boat crew. Six minutes after the collision the Norwegian tramp steamer VOLAND, en route to Windsor, Nova Scotia, plunged beneath the waters of the Sound.

There was great excitement aboard the COMMONWEALTH. J. Howland Gardner was one of the one thousand passengers nearly thrown out of bed by the force of the collision. Gardner raced to the pilothouse. He heard the imploring cries of the VOLAND's crew and saw the ship settling rapidly. Some of VOLAND's crew scrambled up a ladder put over from the COMMONWEALTH. Captain Williamson told the executive that an S O S had been flashed and that COMMONWEALTH's lifesaving crew had lowered their boat. Of especial interest to the ship designer was the first report from below decks that COMMONWEALTH's bow was stove in. Gardner sent a message to Newport to get the spare steamer PURITAN ready to rush to the scene if the COMMONWEALTH was found to be in serious danger.

The eastbound MAINE, New Bedford Line, Captain Harvey H. Webber, only a half mile away, heard the shrieking whistles of the COMMONWEALTH and VOLAND and turned back into the fog even before Williamson's S O S was relayed to her

[3] The wife of VOLAND's Captain Schjott.

[4] "There never was a better sailorman afloat," according to Captain Strickland.

pilothouse. The PROVIDENCE, bound for New York, and the eastbound liners PRISCILLA and PLYMOUTH sped to the disaster spot when the flagship's ominous message crackled through the fog. The Massie Wireless Station at Point Judith spread the alarm ashore.

Gardner and Chief Engineer John V. Sheldon soon determined that the COMMONWEALTH, although badly damaged, could proceed to New York under her own power. Captain Oliver C. Griffin of the PROVIDENCE reported that he would stand by. Williamson radioed to the PRISCILLA and PLYMOUTH and to Newport Repair Shops telling them the PROVIDENCE was at the scene and no assistance would be required. Soon Williamson wirelessed Captain Griffin, "We are in good shape—go ahead." After a two-hour delay, the COMMONWEALTH, a tremendous hole in her bow, moved slowly into the fog. She limped into New York at eleven o'clock. The PROVIDENCE was commissioned in her place and the COMMONWEALTH, a bit over two months in service, went to the dry dock for costly repairs.

At New York news reporters, interviewing COMMONWEALTH passengers, including Navy sailors who had embarked at Newport, touched off a controversy which raged for several days. The sunken VOLAND's crew had been rescued—but by whom? A group of seaman gunners from Newport's Torpedo Station insisted they had lowered a COMMONWEALTH lifeboat and effected the rescue. One weird rumor told of four intoxicated Navy sailors starting a salvage operation of their own by lowering a boat and then becoming lost in the fog, adding to Captain Williamson's sea of troubles. Gardner and Captain Williamson stoutly denied that Uncle Sam's bluejackets had lowered any boats or gone cruising in the fog. They pointed out that COMMONWEALTH's deckhands wore uniforms similar to Navy attire and that uninformed passengers could easily be mistaken in describing the rescue personnel. To this day Strickland, an active participant in the horror of that night, and Haas, a company official, heatedly brand the claim that the Navy made the VOLAND rescue unadulterated bilge.

The vanished VOLAND was well known in New England, having engaged in the Hudson River-Nova Scotia plaster trade for many years. She had been involved in previous accidents. In July 1905, the VOLAND virtually cut the yacht NORMANDIE in two off Dobbs Ferry. Three months later she collided with the anchored schooner ARLEVILLE H. PEARY off the Jersey flats.

The high honor of commanding the world's largest sidewheeler was not a happy experience for Captain Williamson, once a New York policeman, and a thirty-year veteran of the Sound. The steamboat inspectors, blaming COMMONWEALTH for the accident, suspended the skipper's license. He was relieved by Captain William B. Appleby of the PRISCILLA. Appleby handled the COMMONWEALTH with conspicuous success for the next fourteen years. Captain Williamson never came back to the Sound. An Admiralty decision[5] two years later, while criticizing the navigation of the VOLAND "in some respects," fixed the blame on the COMMONWEALTH "because of her excessive speed of 18 knots in dense fog." Williamson, a native of Peconic, Long Island, died in Southold, Long Island, late in 1912 at the age of sixty-five.

Captain Appleby, once described by Albert Haas as "the stateliest captain on the Line," was a boyhood hero of this author. An unposed snapshot[6] of the skipper, about to go on the bridge at New York, led to a long friendship resulting in several free passes and invitations into the skipper's spacious cabin or the pilothouse while under way. To Appleby, who saw thousands of boys every year, the author's name never registered; he was "Bub" to the mariner. Once, when picking up his pass at the purser's window, it was found to be made out to Jack Johnson. Purser Forest W. Simmons laughed, saying "The old man never remembers a name, but it's yours all right. He said a boy would come down for it."

[5] Decision #174F694, 1910.
[6] *The Old Fall River Line*, op. cit., p. 189.

The author now wishes he had been more attentive or inquisitive when Appleby was spinning yarns to him years ago. The COMMONWEALTH skipper had gone through several spine-tingling experiences in his long service on the Sound. One of the most terrifying was the major disaster of 1872,[7] when Appleby was quartermaster on the METIS, en route to Providence. The steamer, in a heavy rain off Watch Hill, collided with the schooner NETTIE CUSHING, from Thomaston, Maine. Preliminary examination disclosed no serious damage to the steamer from the rather light blow, and she continued on her way. Twenty minutes later it was discovered that the METIS was in dire peril. When the steamer sank, Appleby and about fifty others remained on her upper deck, which floated shoreward like a huge raft. For hours survivors came ashore on bits of wreckage. Sad to say, thieves began looting bodies and baggage when word of the disaster spread. Nearly seventy were lost. Appleby was one of the crew of the new Providence Line sidewheeler MASSACHUSETTS, pride of 1877, when she grounded on Long Island.

Considering the size of his ship, the many hazards of the route, and the everlasting fog for which New England is famous, Appleby established an outstanding record in guiding the COMMONWEALTH. One morning, westbound in 1909, because of a tow of barges Appleby was forced to have the COMMONWEALTH go around Mill Rock in Hell Gate. There was a flood tide. He made the turn on the northerly end but the powerful flood tide, boiling into the Harlem River, caught the COMMONWEALTH's port bow and she could not be turned quickly enough to avoid Rylander's Reef. Extensive damage was done to the liner's bottom. Appleby was greatly nettled. A day or two later, after the COMMONWEALTH had been drydocked, Captain Thomas W. Rowland fell in with Appleby on West Street, opposite Pier 18, North River, New York. In what

[7] *Salts of the Sound,* op. cit., p. 175.

he thought was a neighborly manner, Captain Tom casually asked, "Bill, I heard you titched going through the Gate. Much damage done?" Too gentlemanly to retort, "Tom, it's none of your damn business," Appleby said icely, "About an acre of it," and strode angrily away. For years after "Tooting Tom" growled about the way Appleby had cut him short on the West Street sidewalk.

Albert Haas has vivid recollections of a night in April 1910 when the COMMONWEALTH, coming from Fall River, "with every inch of her freight deck jammed," had to veer sharply in the narrow Newport channel to avoid a fishing vessel. She "touched lightly" off Lime Rocks (Ida Lewis) Lighthouse, according to Appleby when he reached Long Wharf a few minutes later. There is only seventeen feet of water in one spot near the lighthouse. A diver was summoned to go down to ascertain the extent of the hull damage. Captain Appleby, hands clasped behind his back, as they were ninety per cent of the time, paced anxiously up and down the wharf. When the diver came up, Appleby hurried toward him and inquired, "Was it sandy where she titched?" "Yes, Captain," responded the underwater explorer as the distraught skipper's face lit up. Pausing for effect, the diver continued, "But, Captain, the grains of sand were pretty damn big–'bout five and a half tons each, I'd say." Appleby sagged.

The COMMONWEALTH in 1908 was officially announced by Mellen to have cost two million dollars. The Roosevelt New Deal era is frequently accused of encouraging newspapers and politicians to add millions or even billions of dollars to every fiscal report. But playing around with figures began years before that time. *Nautical Gazette* of April 21, 1910, telling of the Newport grounding, saluted the COMMONWEALTH as "the *three* million dollar beauty of Long Island Sound."

In dense fog, early in the morning of July 10, 1911, near the spot where she had sunk the VOLAND, the COMMONWEALTH was struck by the fishing steamer JAMES M. GIFFORD. There were striking similarities to the VOLAND accident three years before. As before, the COMMONWEALTH was westbound with a heavy passenger list; weather conditions, locale, and hour were about the same; the PROVIDENCE, Captain Oliver C. Griffin, was again a participant. The COMMONWEALTH was crowded with twelve hundred passengers, nine hundred of whom were traveling to an Elks Convention in Atlantic City. An incredible yarn, depicting Captain Griffin as either a hero or an irresponsible mariner, came out of the affair.

The bow of the fishing vessel, looming up out of the mists, rammed squarely into the port side of the COMMONWEALTH, gashing a sizeable hole in the liner well above the waterline. There was incipient panic on the COMMONWEALTH and passengers in nearby staterooms came rushing out in partial attire. Captain Appleby, not knowing the extent of the damage to the smaller vessel, ordered lifeboats swung out. Quickly the fishing steamer freed herself from the COMMONWEALTH and dropped astern, crossing the bow of the oncoming PROVIDENCE. A cry through the fog, "For God's sake lower a boat—we're sinking," brought action on the PROVIDENCE. Neither Captain Griffin nor Pilot Ezra Daboll realized that there had been a collision several thousand feet ahead. Some reporter, unaware of the practices at sea, concocted the impossible story that Captain Griffin rushed out of the PROVIDENCE's pilothouse and himself went down in her lifeboat to search for the vessel in distress. The ailing GIFFORD was located and revealed that she had struck a big steamer minutes before. Soon the GIFFORD's master reported that his steamer was in no danger of foundering. The COMMONWEALTH, which was hove to, received a reassuring wireless message from Captain Griffin and resumed her voyage to New York. The danger past, the New England Elks regarded the midnight alarm and synthetic shipwreck as a novel interlude to their convention. By the time they reached the Atlantic City conclave the stories about the perils of the deep were probably mighty tall.

Twice, in her early years, the COMMONWEALTH fared badly in fog at The Race. If any landlubber doubts the intensity of the fog that September morning of 1908, when the COMMONWEALTH sent VOLAND to Davy Jones's locker and the cry, "All hands on deck" rang out, let him reflect on this fact—Morse's HARVARD was two hours late in reaching Boston that morning!

C H A P T E R   F O U R

The Iceman Goeth

In 1890 Congress passed the Sherman Antitrust Act forbidding combinations "in restraint of trade." Presidents Harrison, Cleveland, and McKinley did not evidence any particular enthusiasm for enforcing the measure. The Supreme Court rendered no clear-cut decision defining "restraint of trade." Then Theodore Roosevelt, with his big stick and pronouncements against "malefactors of wealth," came to the White House.

The Act apparently meant little to Morgan, Morse, or Mellen, all of whom nurtured ambitious plans for expansion. In 1897, Morse had formed the Consolidated Ice Company. In 1902, Morgan merged the White Star, American, Red Star, Leyland, Atlantic Transport, and Dominion lines into a trans-Atlantic shipping combine, with an aggregate fleet of one hundred and twenty vessels. The financier believed the new International Mercantile Marine would lessen ruinous competition and associate Englishmen and Americans in an enterprise "under American leadership." That same year, the Roosevelt Administration decided to prosecute a Morgan holding company, the Northern Securities Company, for violating the Sherman Antitrust Act. The financial world was appalled. The Sherman statute was considered moribund. On March 14, 1904, the Supreme Court by a 5 to 4 decision declared that the Northern Securities Company was illegal. Nevertheless, the capitalists continued thinking in terms of amalgamations, big business, and national markets.

About the time the HARVARD, YALE, and COMMONWEALTH began churning up the Sound, Morse had his one hundred and twenty million dollar Consolidated Steamship Lines, and Morgan-Mellen, their Consolidated Railway Company. The word "consolidated" was the shibboleth of the hour.[1]

Charles Wyman Morse, candy butcher on a Maine steamboat, successful businessman while yet a college student, lumber dealer, ice mogul, stock manipulator, steamship baron, and large-scale banker, had a genius for the combination of businesses. His exciting life was a fantastic saga of fame and failure, penalty and pardon, wealth and woe.

Morse was born in Bath, Maine, October 21, 1856. His father, Captain Benjamin Wyman Morse, at the age of eighteen, had been given command of a Kennebec River towboat owned by his family. Captain Benjamin established the Knickerbocker Towing Company, one of the largest on the Atlantic Coast, as well as the ice-harvesting firm of B. W. and H. F. Morse.

At an early age, Charles established a reputation for acumen and shrewdness. He attended the public schools of his native city and in 1873 entered Bowdoin College. Shortly before enrolling there, he became bookkeeper for his father, at an annual stipend of $1500. That salary, intended to defray the expenses of his college year, was the seed of his tremendous fortune. Using $500 of it, he hired another young man to do the actual bookkeeping. The remaining $1000 financed his college costs and started him in business.

While a college student, Charles Morse formed a partnership with his cousin, Harry F. Morse. They bought ice from Kennebec River firms and sold it in humid New York City. The collegiate ice purveyor, on one of his first visits to New York City, audaciously called on a leading brewer. Morse came out of the brewery with a signed contract for 50,000 tons of ice. Brashly he asked the millionaire brewer for a credit reference and was sent to a large bank. When Morse returned, the

[1] In 1901 Morgans's banking firm consolidated many concerns into the United States Steel Company, our first billion-dollar corporation.

brewer said, "Young man, I don't know you. You better give me a reference." Morse was forced to confess that he had no New York conections but suggested the brewer telegraph his father in Bath. Captain Benjamin Morse's reply proved his unbounded faith in his son's ability and courage. His wire read, "We don't know where Charlie is or what he is doing, but will back him in anything he does." It is said that Morse and his cousin cleared $50,000 on this one contract. On the day Charles Morse received his diploma he was reputedly worth a half million dollars earned by his own daring and ingenuity!

After leaving college, Morse engaged in business enterprises on a large scale. Pine lands were purchased in the south. His firm, C. W. Morse & Company, with Captain Benjamin, his father, and cousin H. F. Morse as the other principals, supplied lumber to the Bath shipyards and to the New York and Boston market. Ice was sold wholesale in New York, Philadelphia, and southern cities, most of it transported in the firm's own vessels. In 1885 Charles Morse left for New York City, where he really went to town. He suddenly appeared in the financial sky like a meteor, frequently leaving behind him a searing path.

Morse entered the banking field in 1895, when he gained control of the Garfield National Bank. In 1897 he combined twenty-one companies to form the Consolidated Ice Company. On March 11, 1899, Morse incorporated the American Ice Company under the liberal laws of New Jersey, a state which had become cooperative in the formation of "perfectly legal combinations." Despite his long exposure to the political party of Lincoln in rock-ribbed Republican Maine, Morse became friendly with Tammany Hall and especially with New York's Mayor Van Wyck. Indeed, Gotham's chief executive had a financial interest in the Morse ice monopoly.

On a sweltering day in 1900, Morse, now known as "the Ice King," raised the price of ice from thirty cents to sixty cents a hundred pounds. This caused intense suffering in the tenement districts of the stifling city. Newspapers, notably the *New York World*, began a relentless crusade against those who would profit from "blood money of the poor." As a result of the public storm, Morse and "Ice Van Wyck" were forced to reduce the price to its original figure. Stock in the giant combine declined in value and the company ultimately had to be reorganized. Morse, however, was credited with having made a "cool" twelve million dollars out of this manipulation.

Morse, now powerful because of his wealth, realized that he had worked the ice business to the melting point. He owned a fleet of about sixty sailing vessels but yearned to enter the steamship field. Years before, another "Khedive of Wall Street," the notorious Jim Fisk, had become the swaggering admiral of the Fall River Line, which had passed under his control. Morse, never motivated by modest plans, set out to become the "Admiral of the Atlantic coast." His first acquisition was the Eastern Steamship Company, itself an amalgamation of four companies operating between Boston and Maine ports and to the Maritime Provinces.

His second purchase was the Hudson Navigation Company, with night steamers, New York to Albany. Morse was now in the grip of a grandiose passion—to own every coastwise ship on the East coast. In July 1903, Harlan and Hollingsworth, of Wilmington, Delaware, launched the big million-dollar C. W. MORSE for Hudson service.[2] Morse talked of a thirty mile an hour speed for that craft, which prompted *Marine Journal* to suggest, "no one will envy Morse paying the coal bills."

Captain Harold L. Colbeth, who commanded two of the "nautical royalty," Morse's HARVARD and Mellen's MASSACHUSETTS, has fond memories of Morse. Disclaiming any knowledge of Morse's financial dealings, the mariner speaks appreciatively of him as an employer. "He may have been a king down New York way," commented the skipper, "but on the Kennebec you'd never know he was worth a nickel. No airs or fuss about him; he'd come aboard one of his ice boats and sit right down

[2] Was practically same size as PRISCILLA, Fall River Line. Name later changed to FORT ORANGE.

and eat with the crew. Some of them even called him Charlie. He certainly used his help well."

When Morse purchased the Boston-New York Metropolitan Line, revealed plans for his turbine ships, and was known to be in the market for other coastal services, Wall Street gave him more than a superficial glance. In 1907 he bought the Boston Joy Line (steamer OLD DOMINION), which had been gobbled by the New Haven Railroad. Then came the Clyde Line, with a fleet of some twenty ships, serving ports from Boston to Jacksonville. The Mallory Line, from 1866 a cotton carrier, Galveston to New England, was the next link in his aquatic chain. Thirty-five million dollars worth of stocks and bonds were issued against these two lines. Morse's crown as "Ice King" having become a bauble, a new kingdom was readied; Morse was now hailed as the "Steamship King." On February 9, the New Haven Railroad refused his offer of $20,000,000 for its Long Island Sound services. Three days later the news was released that Morse had obtained the Ward Line. The next week it was known that he had the New York and Porto Rico Steamship Company.

By this time Wall Street was amazed. In just one week Morse's transactions in steamship lines had averaged two million dollars a day and he had been refused an offer for ten times that amount! But it wasn't all quiet on the eastern front by any means. Having spurned Morse's offer for the Sound lines, Morgan and Mellen, determining that "steamship lines were essential to the symmetrical development of the New Haven system," went into the market place for additional floating equipment.

A whole battery of Philadelphia lawyers, flanked by a retinue of barristers from Allentown, Bethlehem, Easton, and Harrisburg, would have had difficulty in unraveling the bizarre corporate creations and legerdemain used by the New Haven Railroad as the possessor of steamships.

The "ownership" of the New Haven's steamboats seemed to ebb and flow with the regularity of the tides. The words "complex" and "confusing" hardly do justice to the railroad's corporate structure respecting its marine chattels. To the bewildered public the financial magicians tossed steamer tonnage around with the deftness of vaudeville jugglers.

The steamship maze began innocently enough with the incorporation of the Thompson Tramway Company in 1901, under Special Laws of Connecticut. On January 24, 1902, the Tramway's name was changed to the Worcester and Connecticut Eastern Railway Company. On May 18, 1904, the Superior Court of New Haven County authorized a change in name to the Consolidated Railway Company. Late that year all the New Haven's steamer lines, except the Old Colony Steamboat Company (Fall River Line), were merged under the title, the New England Navigation Company. Late in 1905 the Old Colony Steamboat Company was officially "sold" to the New England Navigation Company. It is respectfully suggested that you mentally file the name "Navigation Company" for future reference. On April 11, 1907, the Consolidated Railway Company purchased all of the steamboat property of the New England Navigation Company for twenty million dollars, giving in payment 200,000 shares of the capital stock of the Consolidated Railway Company.

On May 31, 1907, the New York, New Haven and Hartford Railroad Company was merged with and into the Consolidated Railway Company. The ensuing transactions suggest the financial lawyer's version of "steamboat 'round the bend." On June 1, 1907, the railroad made a contract with the New England Steamship Company[3] for that concern to operate, for thirty years, "all steam and *sailing* vessels" of the New York, New Haven and Hartford Railroad Company. On September 24, the railroad conveyed all of its steamboats and car floats to the New England Steamship Company for $11,353,387.99, taking in payment $11,000,000 in four per cent gold debentures of the steamship company and their demand note for $353,387.99.

[3] Incorporated, state of Connecticut, May 20, 1907.

On January 31, 1908, the New England Steamship Company sold to the New England Navigation Company all its property for $250,000 and assumption of all debts. From February 1, 1908, until June 30, 1912, the New England Navigation Company operated the railroad's steamers.

Then the steamers were again caught in the legalistic whirlpool. On June 27, 1912, the New England Steamship Company bought from the New England Navigation Company all of its physical property. In the agreement covering this purchase the consideration was $14,750,000, $5,750,000 to be paid in cash and the balance in bonds.

So many corporate names came into the picture that even the marine reporters got muddled. An article in *Nautical Gazette* detailing the construction of the railroad's freighters BUNKER HILL, MASSACHUSETTS, and OLD COLONY reported that they were being built for the New Zealand Navigation Company. This prompts the inquiry—was it an honest typographical error or was a marine reporter just being facetious?

At last there was a respite. On December 28, 1917, President Wilson, by wartime proclamation, took possession and control of the New England Steamship Company. Was some puzzled individual heard to mutter, "Thank God!"? During World War I the rail-owned steamer lines were part of the United States Railroad Administration.

If the public was perplexed, what about the steamship employees? For years their popular question was, "Well, whom are we working for this month?" A typical case was that of Frank R. Peabody, for thirty-five years boss painter at the Newport Repair Shops of the New Haven's marine satellite. Toiling constantly at Newport, ostensibly for the same employer, Peabody over the years was carried on these payrolls—The New York, New Haven and Hartford Railroad, Marine District; the New England Navigation Company; the Consolidated Railway Company; the New York, New Haven and Hartford Railroad Company; and the New England Steamship Company.

To confound all the confusion as to who owned what, the

financial pages in September 1907 announced that the heaviest holder of New Haven Railroad securities was the *New England Navigation Company*, with 55,658 shares; J. Pierpont Morgan held the largest individual block, 5077 shares.

Morse, it will be recalled, was grabbing off coastwise and Caribbean lines. Mellen had ideas in that direction, too. It is known that a New Haven plan to establish a steamer line between New England and either Galveston or New Orleans for the transportation of cotton was seriously discussed. But the railroad, through the New England Navigation Company, did secure a coastwise service, the Boston and Philadelphia Steamship Company, a part of the noted Merchants' and Miners' Transportation Company.[4] Familiarly known as the Winsor Line, their seven steamers operated between Boston and Philadelphia; also Providence, Fall River, and Philadelphia. At the time, the New Haven was reported to have paid $2,775,000 for the property; the purchase price was listed as $5,774,500 by the Interstate Commerce Commission some years later. Possession of the Winsor Line gave the New Haven a direct foothold in Philadelphia and the opportunity to establish through rates between Philadelphia and New England.

However, the New Haven's board of directors scuttled one of Mellen's fantastic Long Island Sound schemes. They actually voted down his proposal to operate short-haul freight steamers from New York to such ports as Port Chester, Stamford, and Norwalk. Mellen even threatened to place a fleet of passenger steamers on the Hudson to cripple Morse's New York-Albany night line.

Despite the fact that Morse's new HARVARD and YALE, in September1907, provided "a much needed competition against the New Haven Railroad's monopoly" and were heavily patronized from the start[5], distinctly unhappy days were ahead for

[4] Mellen was elected to the Merchants' and Miners' board of directors.

[5] Captain Colbeth says the HARVARD averaged seven hundred and fifty passengers a night.

the former Ice King. There was an uneasy feeling among business leaders that a severe economic storm was brewing. Morse did not have sense enough to come in out of the rain.

Morse, who then owned "more coastwise tonnage than any other person or corporation," was extremely fortunate in his choice of executive personnel. President of his Consolidated Steamship Lines was the "striking in stature" Calvin Austin, of Maine. Austin's whole life had been in steamboating on the "trying New England coast." He had begun his successful career as office boy for the Sanford Independent Line, later the Boston and Bangor Steamship Company. *Marine Journal* said of Austin that "his brain was as quick and accurate as a stop watch." Captain Harold L. Colbeth called Calvin Austin "a man in a generation." Captain Charles T. Snow, long closely associated with Austin, gave this author equally fervent approval. Calvin Austin's right-hand man in the affairs of the Metropolitan Line was Passenger Traffic Manager Orlando H. Taylor, "universally admired by thousands who have done business with him at the Fall River Line."

Two monopolies—Morse's and Morgan's—met head-on in 1908, one of the luminous years in Long Island Sound history. Marine service between New York and Boston was on a scale undreamed of a few years before. On January 4, Mellen inaugurated the Boston Merchants Line with freighters MASSACHUSETTS, BUNKER HILL, and OLD COLONY.[6] HARVARD and YALE began Metropolitan's first full season of summer passenger service in May. COMMONWEALTH was coming to the Fall River Line in July. According to Mellen, the COMMONWEALTH was "far and away the best boat ever put on the Line—by $500,000, my impression is." Having refused to sell the Fall River Line and affiliated marine properties to Morse, Mellen declared, "I would not sell the trademark of the Fall River Line for $1,500,000 in cash. No other name is advertised the length and breadth of the world better than the Fall River Line."

[6] Discontinued March 19, 1910.

The newspaper advertisements beamed at the eastbound travelers that summer hint at the fervor of the 1908 competition. Basically, the Metropolitan Line offered convenience—a direct, all-water route without the early morning hubbub of Newport docking and freight unloading or "getting up before breakfast" at Fall River to hurry across the gangplank to the Boston train. The Fall River Line fundamental was dependability—one of their punch lines in New York was, "*gets* you to Boston at 8 o'clock next morning." (The Metropolitan, more subject to delay by fog or storm, merely advertised "*Due* Boston at 8 A.M.") The Fall River Line was "a little voyage of contentment"; the Metropolitan promised "a peaceful night on a splendid steamer."

The displays sought to induce action from both sexes by exploiting "extras" and niceties of service. Female patronage was sought for the Metropolitan Line by featuring pens, ink, and writing paper ("Dainty writing rooms for women"); the rival Fall River stressed afternoon tea and music ("Orchestra on each steamer"). Meticulous housekeepers were asked by the Fall River Line to note that "cleanliness is carried to extremes on our steamers." A smoking room and café on the hurricane deck, billed as an "innovation," was expected to attract worldly males to the sister ships HARVARD and YALE. Fall River countered by advising businessmen that the COMMONWEALTH carried a public stenographer and that every effort would be made to "secure special news and stock quotations gratis by wireless." The Fall River Line supplied a miniature tube of Colgate's toothpaste to every stateroom occupant. Both lines had barber shops and tailoring services. Mellen had once complained that "the Fall River Line has been most extravagantly operated; the public has been educated to it and would resent any curtailment." Morse made certain that the public received an even more liberal education.

The proud shipbuilders helped to spread the fame of the popular competing steamers. On the front covers of the leading marine magazine were advertisements of the W. & A.

Fletcher Company and the Quintard Iron Works. For several years the Fletcher space featured an illustration of the HARVARD; often, immediately below, was the Quintard display containing a halftone of either the sidewheeler COMMONWEALTH or the turbine OLD COLONY. Captain Henry O. Nickerson, Fall River Line superintendent, helped reduce the Post Office Department's 1908 deficit by generous mailings of colored post cards of the COMMONWEALTH, created in Germany.

The 1908 record of performance gave the edge to the Metropolitan Line despite the Fall River huckster's honeyed words about dependability and on-time arrivals. During the Metropolitan's season of passenger service, May 11 to November 7, the HARVARD and the YALE *did not miss a trip or meet with an accident.* COMMONWEALTH, on the other hand, had hardly been broken in before she sank the VOLAND, and was forced out of service for several weeks.

At the height of his seeming triumph and public esteem, Morse almost overnight faced a veritable hell on earth. In December 1906 he gave his native city of Bath a "Christmas present" of a contract to the Bath Iron Works for a new 204 stateroom turbine steamer, the CAMDEN,[7] for his Eastern Steamship's Boston-Bangor service. Morse, in the flush days, had been a benefactor to his home city by building it a well-equipped high school. Among the Christmas gifts received by the "Steamship King" on the eve of a most *unhappy* New Year, was a loving cup inscribed:

> "Presented to Charles Wyman Morse, in grateful appreciation of his generosity and public spirit, by the teachers and pupils of Morse High School, Bath, Maine, December 25, 1906."

But the time was not too far distant when Bath was reluctant to extend hospitality to its extraordinary native son!

Mere weeks after his proud liners HARVARD and YALE suc-

[7] As the Colonial Line's COMET, she closed out Sound passenger service, March 1942.

cessfully opened the New York-Boston route, the bottom fell out of everything for Morse. Whether he was superstitious is not known, but the figure thirteen proved disastrous for him. By 1907 Morse controlled thirteen banks.

Morse had been engaging in "stock market adventures" with F. Augustus Heinze, head of the Mercantile National Bank, which involved that institution in ugly rumors. A serious run on that bank resulted, and it appealed to the Clearing House for aid. As a result, the Clearing House demanded the resignation of Heinze and Morse from their banks. On October 20, Morse was forced out as head of the National Bank of North America. There was a general mood of panic; runs started on many banks; the Stock Market was demoralized. The financial world looked to Pierpont Morgan, now a man of three score and ten years, for leadership. Morgan's conspicuous role in the 1907 crisis is graphically described in Frederick Lewis Allen's *The Great Pierpont Morgan.*

While the net earnings of Morse's far-flung Consolidated Steamship Lines seemed substantial—they stood at practically four million dollars for the first nine months of 1907—it was known that Morse had overloaded his giant corporation with an exorbitant weight of capital. His banks had enabled Morse to have ready cash or credit for his sweeping marine purchases. Now his steamship empire was in danger of foundering. Some of Morse's steamship lines reverted to the former owners; others went into the hands of receivers.

In the midst of his financial difficulties Morse disappeared and was finally located in England under the assumed name of Moore. He returned to the United States to face civil and criminal suits. One of the first was from the W. & A. Fletcher Company to enforce a lien for $141,900 held on the HARVARD and YALE.

Morse demonstrated anew his positive flair for profit in the stock market. He dedicated himself to two major objectives —payment of his debts and resistance to all court proceedings. He was pictured in the press as "leading a frugal life" and planning to reorganize his shaky steamship trust. It is said that in a few months he managed to win back several million dollars and to satisfy most of his debts.

In March 1908, a Federal Grand Jury indicted Morse and Alfred H. Curtis, who was Morse's president of the National Bank of North America. They were charged with conspiracy and violating the national banking laws. Specifically, there were three alleged breaches. These were overcertification, misapplication of funds, and false entries in books and reports. The trial of the pair, one of New York's most talked-about events, began on October 14. It was before Judge Hough, in the criminal branch of the United States District Court. The government's case was directed by United States District Attorney Stimson. Morse was represented by an array of distinguished counsel.

Among the interesting facts involving the operation of the National Bank of North America, the government brought out that hundreds of thousands of dollars had been borrowed on personal notes by a $12 a week clerk; that once Morse had a balance of only $1837 but was advanced $100,000; that 4000 shares of American Ice had been purchased under cover of a loan to an individual described as "financially irresponsible." Voluminous testimony was taken concerning the speculation in ice which was called a "base swindle." The name of Calvin Austin, president of the Consolidated Steamship Lines, came into the ice transactions.

When his day in court arrived, Morse, claiming he was "deeply interested in outside ventures" attempted to shift the blame for the bank's failure to Curtis, to whom he said he had left all banking details. Morse asserted that he himself "knew little about banking" and confessed that he "rarely looked at the books of the bank." He introduced the novel defense that he was "only a director and not a practical banker."

Curtis, however, testified that he had not approved of many of Morse's dealings. He produced a strong letter of June 11, 1907, to Morse in which he warned the Wall Street plunger that he was "worried over the situation and realized that the bank's position is anything but safe." He indicated that Morse simply could not imagine that a "financial panic was imminent."

In his summation Charles E. Littlefield, of Morse's counsel, pulled out all the stops in a dramatic four-hour oration. He praised Morse, who had come "from the hills of Maine to the marts of trade," as "neither a coward nor a welcher." He grew sarcastic in telling the attentive jury that "government experts had worn out the books of the bank trying to find something which by ingenuity could be called a crime."

But after three weeks[8] of listening to frequently sensational testimony and the opposing lawyers' forensic appeals, the jury decided that the government had found something "called a crime." Both defendants were found guilty of misapplying the bank's funds, but were acquitted of the charge of conspiracy.

On November 6, in the presence of a crowded courtroom which applauded both judgments, Judge Hough sentenced the once haughty "Ice King" to fifteen years in the federal prison at Atlanta; he suspended a five-year penalty on Curtis. Bail for Morse was refused. As Morse was led to a cell on the seventh floor of Tombs prison he was jeered by a street crowd, many of whom had been embittered by his profits in the household necessity, ice. As the iron gates of the prison closed on Morse the taunt rang out, "How would you like to be the iceman?"

The deflated stock market plunger, stoical in public, broke down in the presence of his family. But when two of his lawyers visited him in Tombs to discuss a bail appeal they found Morse examining bulky mail and "attending to a great deal of business."

On November 10 Morse officially petitioned to be released on bail, claiming that he was now "absolutely penniless." Judge

[8] It was the first time in years a U.S. Court had held sessions on Election Day.

Hough protested granting any bail, but a higher tribunal subsequently freed Morse[9] on the posting of a $125,000 guarantee.

Morse assuredly did not lack faith in himself, or the native ability to make dollars beget dollars. While out on bail he again became an active figure in Wall Street. He was elected to the presidency of the Metropolitan Steamship Company while his appeal from Judge Hough's sentence was being weighed. In a few months time Morse was reported to have recouped several million dollars!

Finally the court decree came—the iceman goeth. Morse began his servitude at Atlanta on January 3, 1910. From that day on, the discredited speculator began an unrelenting battle to regain his freedom.

The incarceration of Morse appears to have met with widespread approval at the time. A typical editorial comment was that of the influential magazine *The Outlook*.[10] Ascribing to the reckless Morse a major role in causing the panic of 1907, they said, "The conviction and sentencing of Charles W. Morse will have a most salutary effect upon the country. It will indicate that the federal government does not administer one kind of justice for a defaulting bank clerk and another kind for a dishonest bank owner." In similar vein the *Marine Journal* expressed "keen regret that the methods of high finance were ever applied to the American shipping business."

The uncertain days of 1907, when the financial world stood on the brink of ruin, was a measuring rod of men. J. Pierpont Morgan, marshalling every resource, virtually functioning as a one-man central banking system, was hailed for his spirit of confidence and untiring leadership. Charles Wyman Morse, his Long Island Sound rival, was held by many to be answerable for the collapse of important financial institutions and their tragic aftermath.

[9] January 17, 1909.
[10] Issue of November 14, 1908.

CHAPTER FIVE

The Nation's Greatest Maritime Spectacle

Marine men were grateful for the coming of a constructive event of international magnitude. The 1909 Hudson-Fulton Celebration was an antidote to the unhealthy conditions resulting from the machinations of Morse and his kind. The panic of 1907, largely induced by the "rough, red rogues of Wall Street," had brought receiverships and reorganizations to many prominent steamship lines. It was the era in which a schoolboy, when asked, "Who created the world?" replied, "God did, but it was reorganized by James J. Hill, J. Pierpont Morgan, and John D. Rockefeller."

The autumn of 1909 marked the three-hundredth anniversary of the discovery of the Hudson River by Henry Hudson and the somewhat belated centennial of Robert Fulton's successful inauguration of steam navigation on that lordly stream.

An elaborate series of ceremonies and pageants was planned to commemorate these most important events in maritime history. It was to be the most extensive festival since the dedications of the Brooklyn Bridge in May 1883, and of the magnificent buildings of the World's Columbian Exposition at Chicago a decade later.

The nautical phases of the jubilee were placed in charge of Captain Jacob W. Miller, general manager of the Fall River Line, and Captain George A. White, of the Hudson River Day Line. Both officials had rich backgrounds in engineering and navigation. Miller, the son of United States Senator J. W. Miller, of New Jersey, was born in 1847, the year the Fall

River Line began its distinguished service. He graduated from Annapolis in 1867 and subsequently engaged in canal building in Nicaragua.[1] After leaving naval service he became manager of the Providence and Stonington Steamship Company. On the death of Captain Stephen A. Gardner (father of J. Howland Gardner) in 1899, Miller was made the general superintendent of the New Haven Railroad's consolidated steamer lines. White, a civil engineer, had entered the service of the Lake Champlain Transportation Company in 1877. Seven years later he became purser for the Hudson River Day Line and then went into the pilothouse as skipper of their steamers ALBANY and HENDRICK HUDSON.

To dramatize the extraordinary advances in ship construction and motive power as represented by the LUSITANIA, the HARVARD, and the COMMONWEALTH, pride of their respective types in 1909, exact replicas were built of Hudson's tiny HALF MOON and Fulton's crude steam-propelled CLERMONT. These replicas were the focal point for the whole celebration.

Months in advance of the observance, Miller and White shaped plans for a mammoth marine parade to take place late in September. Week after week the shipping pages overflowed with breath-taking announcements of the participation of United States and foreign war vessels as well as hundreds of American steamboats. At the outset it was planned to have the COMMONWEALTH, "largest steamboat in the world," glistening in the newness of her second season, act as the flagship and venture into the upper reaches of the Hudson. Finally, it was determined that, because of her size and the heavy travel expected from New England, the COMMONWEALTH and her older consort, the PRISCILLA, should remain in active Fall River Line service. The recognition went to the four-year-old sister, the PROVIDENCE, last Fall River Line passenger ship designed by the noted George Peirce. The magnitude of the celebration's

[1] Miller retired from the Fall River Line, 1909, to assist in constructing the Cape Cod Canal.

crowning feature, the naval parade, was indicated six weeks before the event by *Marine Journal's* announcement that "not a single licensed passenger steamer remains unchartered, New England to Norfolk." Line after line advertised that its steamers would carry passengers to view the unprecedented spectacle. The Fall River Line assigned the PURITAN, PLYMOUTH, CITY OF LOWELL, RICHARD PECK, and BRIDGEPORT to the spectator fleet at $5.00 a person.

For weeks the front-page news in New York and environs dealt with the projected events in the forthcoming "World's Fair condensed in a week" as the *New York Sun* called the Hudson-Fulton Celebration. Normally, the talk of the town would be such exciting items as the rival claims of the impostor, Dr. Cook, and the heroic explorer, Admiral Robert E. Peary, that they had discovered the North Pole; the Cunarders LUSITANIA and MAURETANIA had within days broken their own trans-Atlantic speed records; two girls had successfully swum dangerous Hell Gate. But fifty energetic Hudson-Fulton committees were capturing headlines by revealing their plans for the assemblage of warships, aeroplane flights by Wilbur Wright and Glenn H. Curtiss,[2] electrical displays to give the radiance of twenty-six million candles, spectacular land parades, and the stupendous water procession honoring the re-created HALF MOON and the CLERMONT. Summing it up the *New York Sun* said, "No celebration has so excited New York."

Two tragic events occurred on the eve of the festivities. On August 30, the NORWICH,[3] "the world's oldest steamboat" (built in 1836 and still active in 1909) burned at Rondout, New York. She was slated to have a conspicuous place in the first division of the naval parade. Soon afterward, Charles Kenneth Moore, grandnephew of Robert Fulton, who, days before, had been a guest on the trial trip of the replica CLER-

[2] A feature was "an attempt" to fly from New York to Albany.

[3] Operated on Long Island Sound for fifteen years; then 65 years as Hudson River towboat.

MONT, committed suicide. He swallowed poison an hour after writing a letter to the celebration committee asking, "What provision has been made for relatives of Robert Fulton?"

The commemoration was a bonanza for steamboat owners. The arrival of scores of warships from abroad in late September was the signal for an afternoon fireworks display. Daylight bombs released hundreds of small flags as thousands lined the shores or sailed the Hudson on numerous spectator craft. A full page of "Sail Around the Warships" advertisements, at prices from $2.00 to $6.00, appeared in the New York dailies. Piers and buildings along the New York and New Jersey shores were beautifully decorated. The illumination at night was so brilliant that "the moon looked as if ashamed of herself."

Steamboat veterans and landlubber showmen had been sure that New York's welcome to triumphant Admiral Dewey would never be surpassed by any other day of homage. They doubted that more types or sizes of ships could ever float on the Hudson at one time, more miles of bunting snap in the salt-laden breeze, or more brilliant fireworks consort with the stars than had marked the gala holiday of September 1899, honoring the hero of Manila. But as the midnight hour tolled on Saturday, September 25, 1909, all freely admitted that the "morning, noon, and night" water pageant of the Hudson-Fulton Celebration would go down in history as the unqualified greatest.

How many millions participated in the "roaring day for two tiny ships" will never be known. Neither the police nor the transit lines could handle the crowds. According to the *New York Sun* "it was a great day for taxicabs."

There were sixteen hundred guests of the commission aboard the flagship PROVIDENCE, in charge of "Admiral" George A. White, when the proud Sound liner cast off for Staten Island where the HALF MOON and the CLERMONT were moored. The HALF MOON almost spoiled the show by ramming lightly into the CLERMONT off the St. George ferry landing but no harm resulted. At 1:15 P.M., "Admiral" White gave orders for the Fall River liner to lead the big parade. The HALF MOON was towed by the tug FRED B. DALZELL; the CLERMONT lumbered under her own power. For hours, division after division of steam vessels moved through the Hudson without a hitch. It was a tribute to the organizing ability of Captain Miller and the vessel commanders.

Honorable though her position was, leading the Hudson-Fulton flotilla may have been the slowest voyage the PROVIDENCE ever sailed. Once, when she fell out of line and passed the CLERMONT with her giant paddles revolving at a mere six miles per hour, the PROVIDENCE was reported as "whizzing by" the replica. Wigwag experts transmitted sailing orders and greetings from the top deck of the PROVIDENCE. Prominent mention was made of the fact that wireless messages were dispatched to and from the flagship PROVIDENCE. The nation had come a long way since Fulton's epochal voyage!

The names of the seven steamboats in the parade's first division will bring tears to the eyes of steamboat lovers. All have gone to the boneyard. The flagship PROVIDENCE was followed by the sidewheeler HENDRICK HUDSON, then the largest of the Hudson River Day Line fleet. Next in order came the popular Hudson River steamers; ROBERT FULTON, RENSSELAER[4], and ALBANY. The twin-screw CITY OF LOWELL of the New Haven Railroad's New England Navigation Company finished off the first group because the ancient NORWICH had been swept by flames a month earlier. Famous steamers in the second division were the propeller NORTH STAR, Maine Steamship Company; C. W. MORSE, Hudson Navigation Company; CHESTER W. CHAPIN, New England Navigation Company; PLYMOUTH, Fall River Line, and the CITY OF WORCESTER, once hailed as "the belle of Long Island Sound."

It was only a half-century ago that the PROVIDENCE, sub-

[4] She and the Day Line's FULTON came out new the year of the Celebration.

stituting for the COMMONWEALTH, steamed at the head of a Hudson River steamboat procession in tribute to Robert Fulton. Never again can such a stirring maritime spectacle be witnessed!

C H A P T E R   S I X

'Round the Cape — to Frisco!

A prophet addressed the New England Dry Goods Association in Boston on February 11, 1908. Louis Dembitz Brandeis, a native of Louisville, but who, from 1879, had been known in Boston as "one of its most brilliant legal minds," was the speaker. He sought to arouse Massachusetts business leaders to the perils of a transportation monopoly.

There was awareness, premonition, and urgency in his stirring message. Summarizing the New Haven Railroad's steamship transactions, Brandeis said:

> "The New Haven has suppressed all competition between Boston and New York. . . . The Joy Line of steamers arose but soon passed under New Haven control. The Enterprise Line began operating between New York and Fall River; New York and Providence, with good promise of success. The New Haven, under secret cover of the Neptune Line, entered upon fierce competition. Last October (1907) the Enterprise succumbed. There is not a single independent line of steamers between Massachusetts and New York except the Metropolitan Line; now it has passed into the hands of a receiver. May we not expect to see as the next step its fine steamers HARVARD and YALE flying the New Haven flag, and the last vestige of steamship competition disappear?"

The world has wrestled with many unanswerable questions such as "Who killed Cock Robin?" or "How old is Ann?" New England has a baffler, too. Did Charles Sanger Mellen have anything to do with the eviction of the steamers HARVARD and YALE?

In one of the many federal governmental investigations of the tangled affairs of the New Haven Railroad, Mellen was asked the leading question, "Did the New Haven or any of its subsidiaries acquire the HARVARD and YALE at any time?" Innocently, the rail executive replied, "*I never knew* but I do not believe we ever had one dollar's interest in them at any time."

Well, possibly Mellen "never knew" if the New Haven acquired the collegiate duo, but unless he had a convenient lapse of memory he knew they could have done so. Government investigators found copious evidence in the files at the New Haven's sprawling Yellow Building. For instance, late in October 1907[1] a memorandum from a subordinate official informed Mellen that a Pacific coast organization (represented by Thomas McGovern of New York) wished to purchase the HARVARD and YALE and were anxious to learn "if the New Haven is sufficiently interested in the removal of the competition to take about seven hundred thousand dollars worth of securities." The report also advised that "the Metropolitan Line can now be purchased at a reasonable figure . . . we could make it appear that the Line has fallen back into original hands and not publicly connect the New Haven with the transaction." Mellen affixed these words on the bottom of the memorandum: "I would not buy anything now, nor put up a dollar on any such scheme."

But the subject was not closed. On November 13, 1907, when the heat was on Morse, Stevenson Taylor dispatched a note to Mellen confirming arrangements for a meeting of Morse, Mellen, and himself at Grand Central Terminal the next day. Taylor informed Mellen that Morse was "not desirous of selling the Eastern or Metropolitan lines and goes back to the proposition of getting out of the passenger business between New York and Boston. *I discouraged the idea of your*

[1] Morse's financial affairs were then becoming involved.

COMMONWEALTH—keel to truck. Unusual photo of massive Sound liner in dry dock

Charles S. Mellen,
New Haven R. R.
President

Charles W. Morse,
"Ice and Steamship
King"

J. Pierpont Morgan,
powerful financier,
New Haven's
backer

Calvin Austin, "down east"
steamboater

Louis D. Brandeis, Boston
anti-merger lawyer

MONOPOLISTS AND THEIR FOE

INAUGURATION OF PASSENGER SERVICE BETWEEN

NEW YORK and BOSTON

Wednesday, Sept. 18th, 1907

Metropolitan Line Express Steel Triple Turbine

Steamships YALE and HARVARD

The Metropolitan Steamship Company is pleased to announce the inauguration of Passenger Service by its **Direct All Water Route** between New York and Boston, via Long Island Sound and the Atlantic Ocean, on Wednesday, Sept. 18th, 1907.

Schedule. Leave New York from Pier 45, North River, foot of West 10th Street, week days and Sundays, at 5 P. M., due Boston at 8 o'clock the next morning. Same service in the opposite direction. From Boston steamers will leave South Side India Wharf.

The Yale and Harvard are the fastest and most luxuriously fitted passenger Steamships in America. Nothing contributable to the comfort, convenience and entertainment of passengers has been omitted in the construction of these great steamships. Fine dining room service. Music. Lounging and Reading Rooms for men. Dainty Writing Rooms. Sumptuous Staterooms with or without bath.

Tickets and staterooms from New York, also from Boston, at 290 Broadway, Telephone 1000 Worth; Pier 45, N. R., Telephone 6580 Spring, and at principal Tourist and New York Transfer Company offices throughout Greater New York.

Express Freight Service. Best route for the transportation of Automobiles between New York and Boston.

1907 steamer ads vied for patronage. Right: YALE's "dainty writing room"

HOPPE'S BAND AND ORCHESTRA

STANISLAW HOPPE, DIRECTOR AND MANAGER

28 Seasons on the Fall River Line

Established Fall River Line met challenge with stress on music

BOSTON and Points in NEW ENGLAND

FALL RIVER LINE for Newport, Fall River, Boston, and all Eastern and Northern points. Steamers PRISCILLA and PURITAN. Orchestra on each. Leave Pier 19, N. R., foot Warren Street, weekdays and Sundays at 5.30 P. M.

PROVIDENCE LINE, for Providence, Boston, East and North. Leave Pier 18, North River, foot of Murray street, week-days only 6.00 P. M. Steamers PROVIDENCE and PLYMOUTH (New). Orchestra on each.

NEW BEDFORD LINE, for New Bedford, Woods Hole, Oak Bluffs, Nantucket, Mattapoisett, Marion and other points on Cape Cod. Strs. MAINE and NEW HAMPSHIRE leave Pier 40, N. R., foot Clarkson St. week-days only at 6.00 P. M.

NORWICH LINE for New London, Norwich, Stonington, Worcester, East and North. Strs. CITY OF LOWELL and CHESTER W. CHAPIN leave Pier 40 N. R., foot Clarkson St., week-days only, 5.00 P. M., foot of East 22d St., 6.30 P. M.

NEW HAVEN LINE for New Haven, Hartford, Springfield and North. Str. RICHARD

Interior views, Morse's twin vessels HARVARD and YALE. Top: Entrance lobby; Grand stairway. Center: Grand Salon and gallery. Bottom: Spacious Dining Room

New Haven's three fast freighters were converted into luxurious passenger ships. Photos of Old Colony show Lobby and Dining Room (left); Grill Room and bedroom with bath

Giants of their class! Coastal COMMONWEALTH (456 ft. long), left side of New York pier; LEVIATHAN, U.S. Lines, (907 ft. long) in river

The "Leviathan of Long Island Sound"—broad, long and high. Stern view of COMMONWEALTH at Fall River Wharf

New Haven Railroad denied responsibility for sudden transfer of competing YALE and HARVARD to Pacific coast in 1910. Duo became popular there

Above: Sleek YALE at San Diego

Left: Wreck of HARVARD, which stranded near Santa Barbara, 1931

G. H. Williamson

W. B. Appleby

E. R. Geer

R. M. Robinson

Daniel Barrett

N. L. Strickland

F. H. Avery

COMMONWEALTH COMMANDERS 1908-1937

wanting the HARVARD and YALE. Morse is profuse in expressions of wanting to do *what you wish* on these lines, like meeting you on rates. Of course, he wants no fight. Today's stock market and business prospects will interfere with his projects."

Copies of correspondence found at New Haven were proof positive that negotiations concerning the Morse steamers was not unfinished business. On January 15, 1908, Benjamin Campbell, New Haven's traffic vice president, in a letter to Mellen, suggested how the railroad might operate the speedy passenger ships or Metropolitan freighters "without running against public policy." Campbell's solution was that they be controlled by the "seemingly independent" Neptune Line, the railroad's "cheap line," New York to Fall River. Mellen was told, "McGovern can place the HARVARD and YALE with Pacific coast parties for two million dollars if he can find some way of disposing of the other four Metropolitan steamers."[2]

About this same time it was revealed that the New Haven was urging the construction of the six million dollar Cape Cod Canal, connecting Buzzards and Barnstable bays. The August Belmont Company was the financial backer of the Boston, Cape Cod, and New York Canal Company. The proposed inside waterway would eliminate seventy miles of dangerous and frequently fog-bound waters. Two decades later the New Haven probably wished it had never given its blessing to the project. Use of the Cape Cod Canal by the New York-Boston liners of the competing Eastern Steamship Lines on a year-round basis was an important factor in the decline of the Fall River Line.

The years 1907 and 1908 were undoubtedly the most frenzied in the history of New England transportation. There was dramatic news most every day from every front. Rumblings and rumors concerning the future of Morse's new HARVARD

[2] Freighters H. F. DIMOCK, H. M. WHITNEY, JAMES S. WHITNEY, and HERMAN WINTER.

and YALE continued. Late in 1907, Mellen's fast freighter MASSACHUSETTS, built to compete with Morse, was reduced to carrying freight to Bridgeport. On January 4, 1908, the fight against Morse really began. Mellen opened the Boston Merchants Line (freight) with the MASSACHUSETTS and BUNKER HILL at rates twenty-five per cent less than those prevailing. A month later Morse's Consolidated Steamship Lines went into the hands of a receiver. In March, as detailed in a preceding chapter, Morse and banker Curtis were indicted. On May 22, to the joy of the crusading Brandeis and the consternation of Mellen, the federal government filed a petition to separate the New Haven Railroad from its interstate trolley lines and to thwart its attempt to gain control of the Boston and Maine Railroad. Mellen was astounded at this development because he was known to "stand well with President Theodore Roosevelt" and was reported to have received assurance that no Department of Justice action against the New Haven was probable. Two months later cannons boomed and whistles shrieked as "Mellen's apartment-house boat", COMMONWEALTH, became the Fall River Line flagship. On November 6, Morse heard the ominous words that he was sentenced to Atlanta prison. Once during the year, absence of cash by his Consolidated Steamship Lines led the sheriff to Pier 32, North River, New York, with an attachment to satisfy a $100,000 judgment.

A plan to "save the Eastern and Metropolitan lines from complete financial wreck" was consummated in the United States Circuit Court, Portland, Maine, on November 25. The Eastern Steamship Company petitioned for approval to borrow $1,100,000 from Hayden Stone & Company to liquidate all claims against the Eastern. The move by the Boston bankers was considered an attempt to "freeze out Morse."

While the financiers and lawyers wrestled with the reorganization problems, the HARVARD and YALE operated under the Metropolitan flag during the summer season of 1908. The company's annual report showed that the two popular passenger liners produced a net profit of $400,000 but the year-round freighters, no doubt affected by the Mellen opposition, were about $100,000 in the red. Accidents to the rival New York-Boston steamers made news, too. Early in March 1909 the MASSACHUSETTS, at full speed, ran over the rocks at Middle Ground and went ashore in Lambert Cove, near Cedar Tree Neck. J. Howland Gardner's unique design of the MASSACHUSETTS, with her boilers in two separate compartments, was justified when rocks tore the vessel's outer hull from the bow compartment to the after engine room bulkhead and lifted the forward boilers up to the main deck. The serious accident to the MASSACHUSETTS had the Newport Repair Shops as well as the navigators in a dither for days afterward. Albert Haas was one of the officials who manned the freight steamer BOSTON, taking a crew of longshoremen out to the stranded steamer to unload her cargo. But alas, the BOSTON came afoul of the frowning rocks and had to steam to New York for repairs without being able to remove so much as one crate from the MASSACHUSETTS. The Merritt-Chapman & Scott Company, assisting on the salvage job, fared little better. Their well-known tug TASCO also struck the Middle Ground, damaging her rudder and wheel. The Arbuckle Wrecking Company effectively used compressed air to enable men to patch holes in the freighter's steel hull. After she was pulled off the beach, her forward boilers under water, drawing twenty-two feet forward and fourteen feet aft, the wounded MASSACHUSETTS proceeded to dry dock under steam from the four after boilers. Captain "Handsome Harry" Barrett and First Officer W. T. Holmes were tried by the steamboat inspectors at Boston, charged with "inattention to duty" and "careless navigation in fog." Holmes was ruled responsible for the improper course being steered and his license was suspended for fifteen days. On June 4, as a result of a collision, the YALE badly damaged the Hoboken ferry BERGEN.

The fast HARVARD was but a "jump ahead" of destruction when a four-alarm, noon-hour fire on Saturday, July 16, 1910, destroyed Pier 14, North River, New York. The Metropolitan Line had occupied the big Fulton Street pier about a month.[3] Freighter H. F. DIMOCK, loading on the north side of the former Red Star Line pier, had most of her superstructure burned off before tugs hauled her out into the stream and fireboats drowned out the flames. A "chuckle-headed longshoreman," disobeying rules by smoking a pipe on the river end of the dock, was responsible for the conflagration, which in minutes was destroying lighters, coal barges, and freight and roaring toward West Street. The white paint of the HARVARD began to blister as her whistle wailed for aid from river tugs, and Captain Lorenzo H. Crowell implored the engineers for power to move away from the inferno. As steam was hastily gotten up, inky smoke belched from the HARVARD's stack,[4] causing many to believe that she, too, was ablaze. New York's Fire Chief Croker saw at once that saving Pier 14 was "the job of an arch-angel." For a time the Lackawanna ferry slip and Washington Market were threatened.

On the busy pier's second floor, Paymaster W. A. Huntington was dispensing salary envelopes. He thought he had time to finish disbursing, but was finally forced to toss three thousand dollars in bills and coin into two satchels and flee for his life. His wild dash was interrupted by a policeman, who felt certain the laden sprinter had looted the pier's safe. After proper identification, Huntington was escorted to Pier 9, North River, former Metropolitan Line headquarters. Some weeks later the marine underwriters, who were carrying a million dollars[5] on the HARVARD, presented five-hundred dollar purses to Captain Crowell, First Officer W. T. Holmes and Chief Engineer L. D. Moseley in recognition of their efforts in saving the passenger liner.

[3] Pier 14, North River, was later used by the Fall River Line from November 28, 1912, until termination of service, 1937.

[4] Had recently been equipped with oil fuel; quick firing resulted.

[5] Insurance was underwritten by sixty companies, fifty of them British.

Reorganization and rumor—that was the fare placed before news-hungry financial and marine reporters during 1909. Was Morse in or out of the troubled Metropolitan Line? Had the HARVARD *and* YALE been sold? If so, was the purchaser the New Haven Railroad or a company thousands of miles away? In April, the speed queens were advertised to resume New York-Boston service, "disposing of the story they were recently sold to the Pacific coast." In June, ex-Governor William T. Cobb of Maine, Calvin Austin, and A. I. Culver, receivers, announced preliminary plans for the reorganization of the Metropolitan Line. By September there was a well-founded opinion that the New Haven Railroad was seeking to snare the Metropolitan, which was to be sold at auction in October. One New Haven director was reported to have said, "I am sure Mr. Mellen has no authority for buying the Metropolitan Line. I do not think he is buying an interest for himself." A yarn had Mellen and Morse taking over the company jointly. To a newshawk's query Morse responded, "When a man is going to an auction he doesn't usually announce beforehand that he is a buyer." A most significant announcement late in September was the word that the New England Navigation Company (New Haven owned) would soon discontinue its Boston-New York Merchants Line fast freight service, "leaving the field open to the Metropolitan Line."

In Boston on October 9, John W. McKinnon, a Chicago banker, bid $2,500,000[6] for the Metropolitan at a foreclosure sale. It was obvious that the new Metropolitan remained in Morse's hands because, when McKinnon handed in the check, it was announced that Morse would serve as president, McKinnon as vice president, and that the "hailing port" of the reorganized company would be Morse's home city, Bath, Maine. It was stated that the HARVARD and YALE "would run as long as the service paid."

[6] Nine thousand less than mortgage held by the American Trust Company.

Deeds formally transferring the property of the Metropolitan Steamship Company of Maine to the reorganized Metropolitan Steamship Company of New Jersey were passed in Boston on November 24. At that time the public was informed that Morse would hold "no official position in the reorganized company." Subsequently, these two Metropolitan companies, sometimes called "Metropolitan Steamship Company No. 1" and "Metropolitan Steamship Company No. 2," engaged in a mysterious game of financial tag—nobody knew just who was "it." And Mellen was in the game, too!

In January 1910, a Pacific coast steamship company denied it had been negotiating for the purchase of the HARVARD and YALE, which they claimed "were not entirely suitable for Pacific coast business." But in September, with startling abruptness, the steamers were withdrawn from New York-Boston service and announced to make a long journey to a new home port on the Pacific.

Two pronouncements early in March had financial and marine reporters sniffing the salt-laden breeze for an aquatic rat. A new corporation was organized in Maine to take over the steamers and business of the Metropolitan Steamship Company of New Jersey. A law firm was the "nominal purchaser." Coincident with the news from the Pine Tree state came word from Mellen that the Boston Merchants Line would be immediately discontinued. This gave credence to the rumors that the New Haven Railroad had secured control of the new Metropolitan Steamship Company of Maine. Calvin Austin, president of the Eastern Steamship Company, was named as chief of the new Metropolitan concern, and burst into the press with the statement that "the New Haven Railroad does not control the new corporation but it is hoped to have friendly relations with them." Astute editors, certain that the New Haven had absorbed its competitor trumpeted, "Boston Steamship Rivalry Ends."

On May 23, the renovated HARVARD and YALE began their

third[7] summer season on the direct Boston run, "recognized as the most popular route between the two cities." A few days before, YALE, with scores of guests aboard, made a "trial trip" to Ambrose Lightship to try out the new oil fuel and to show off the many additional private bath bedrooms. The number of private baths on the Morse steamers far exceeded those on Mellen's highly touted COMMONWEALTH. The liquid fuel "worked very satisfactorily." The advertising men pointed out that, on the Metropolitan, voyagers would not be wiping cinders from their eyes or hair. Leaving time from Pier 9, North River, was fixed at 4 P.M. to afford travelers "an opportunity to view the enchanting scenery at sunset." The fare to Boston was $4.00. In a month, a timetable revision restored the 5 P.M.[8] sailing hour and the Metropolitan transferred its terminal to Pier 14, North River.

Mariners had given the HARVARD and YALE a good name as sea boats; they had transported hundreds of thousands around rampaging Cape Cod in heavy weather. But the sudden news in September 1910 that they had been sold to a corporation on the Pacific coast, "the name of which is shrouded in mystery,"[9] and would sail around Cape Horn to California caused head-shaking aplenty. Standing alone the epoch-making coast to coast voyage of the HARVARD and YALE entitles them to high rank among America's nautical royalty!

The hazardous journey, now in fact after three years of gossip, presented many technical problems. The fast liners had opened the 1910 season as oil burners, then a rarity. Few ports in the United States or South America could replenish that fuel. Consequently, the steamers had to be partially reconverted to coal. It was arranged that they would steam some 5000 miles using oil and then the forward boilers, altered to burn coal, would take over. On the Pacific coast they were to

[7] Service in 1907 was only for a few weeks.
[8] Fall River Line left New York at 5:30 P.M.
[9] Pacific Navigation Company.

be converted back to oil. In anticipation of rough going the sides were sheathed and the joiner work strengthened.

The pair left New York for California late in October and almost immediately were buffeted by a West Indies hurricane. Steaming in sight of each other all the way through some of the world's busiest waters they reached San Pedro on December 16, after putting in at several ports, including Rio. They were said to be the first turbine ships to pass through the Straits of Magellan. (Later when called into war service in 1918 both steamers sailed through the Panama Canal to and from the English Channel.)

Interestingly enough, Morse's speeders were not the only Sound steamers to go to the Pacific. The Enterprise Line's much smaller ST. CROIX sailed from New York, January 30, 1908, and on arriving on the West Coast must have felt right at home. Reminiscent of her spirited Fall River competition, she engaged in a rate war, operating San Francisco to Los Angeles at a $1.00 fare. In November 1909, she burned to the water's edge. The idle ex-Joy Line's KENTUCKY was made ready at Hoboken to take her place. However, her wooden hull could not stand the strain of the Atlantic's heavy weather and she foundered on February 4, 1910. Prompt response to her S O S by the Mallory Line's ALAMO saved her crew of forty-six.

Pacific coast marine scribes became as enthusiastic over the performance of the Morse pair as had their Atlantic brethren. On an early trip, San Francisco to San Pedro, the YALE "broke all records" by steaming through open seas for a bit over sixteen hours at 21.72 knots.

The HARVARD and YALE had hardly reached the distant Pacific than Mr. Mellen was heard from. The New Haven Railroad would establish an all-water passenger line, New York to Boston! How could anybody (except possibly a Brandeis) believe the New Haven had anything to do with the disappearance of the popular HARVARD and YALE? The railroader waxed indignant at any such suggestion. "The steamers HARVARD and YALE are owned by the Metropolitan Steamship Company of

New Jersey, in which concern neither the New Haven nor any of its directors has an interest to the extent of a single dollar," explained Mellen to the doubters, whose number was legion. "The New Haven has no part or parcel in the transferring of these steamers," he concluded.

Speaking in dulcet tones dedicated to the public welfare, Mellen then proclaimed, "But the New Haven has undertaken to supply the city of Boston, as soon as possible, with other steamers and an equivalent service, which it hopes will prove as satisfactory as the HARVARD and YALE." How magnanimous!

There was no fooling about it! On November 21, the New Haven announced that its crack freighters BUNKER HILL, MASSACHUSETTS, and OLD COLONY would be converted to luxurious passenger liners and would replace their erstwhile "enemies" HARVARD and YALE. William Cramp and Sons, Philadelphia, builders of the COMMONWEALTH, received the $1,500,000 contract for stripping the trio to the hulls and constructing new superstructures. Haas has a February 1908 memorandum from Gardner to Stevenson Taylor which reads, "According to instructions of February 7 from C. S. Mellen we are to make plans for placing passenger accommodations on the BUNKER HILL, MASSACHUSETTS, and OLD COLONY." There were to be 186 staterooms, sixteen of which were to be deluxe parlor rooms, six to contain private baths. With "free berths," sleeping accommodations were to be provided for a total of 612 passengers. Early in 1911 the Maine Steamship Company, which everybody knew was controlled by the New Haven, officially took over the three ships. The BUNKER HILL and MASSACHUSETTS were to be operated New York-Boston by the "Maine Steamship Company-Metropolitan Line"; the OLD COLONY, New York to Maine, by the "Maine Steamship Company-Portland Line."

Laymen would find the complicated financial dealings of the New Haven Railroad and the Eastern Steamship Company about as understandable as the Einstein theory. Before Christmas of 1911, there was a steamship reorganization under the laws of Maine. As a result, the Eastern Steamship Company, controlling practically all steamer services east of Cape Cod, the New Haven's Maine Steamship Company, and the Metropolitan Line became the Eastern Steamship Corporation. The new organization promised extensive alterations to the BUNKER HILL and MASSACHUSETTS for the summer of 1912. The ships would henceforth burn oil and be equipped with fire-sprinkler systems like Fall River's COMMONWEALTH. The luxury items included additional staterooms, enlarged main deck dining rooms and a café on the hurricane deck. All inside staterooms were to be equipped with electric fans, "a decided innovation."

Suffice it to say that Mellen's ex-freighters, now glistening white, were worthy successors to Morse's departed turbine liners. An old record at Boston shows that for a three-week period in August 1912, the BUNKER HILL and MASSACHUSETTS averaged 15 hours, 20 minutes coming from New York. Their tight schedule called for sixteen hours.

A stark tragedy in the North Atlantic on Sunday night, April 14, 1912, had a profound effect on safety measures on Long Island Sound steamers. The "unsinkable" TITANIC, pride of J. Pierpont Morgan's[10] International Mercantile Marine, went down with a loss of 1517 lives, due to insufficient lifeboats. Mellen and J. Howland Gardner moved immediately to insure that the heavily traveled Fall River Line, with its enviable safety record, could never have such a calamity. The New Haven's directors voted a quarter of a million dollars to equip the New England Nagivation Company steamers with the latest and best lifeboat equipment. The "largest order placed at one time in the United States for lifeboat equipment" was given to the Welin Marine Equipment Company for 191 lifeboats and 108 life rafts. The COMMONWEALTH was provided with 28 lifeboats and 24 rafts, with a total capacity of 1656 persons; boatage on the PRISCILLA after the TITANIC disaster was

[10] There were some unfounded charges that economies dictated by Morgan were responsible for the disaster.

for 1605 persons. A large order was also placed by the Eastern Steamship Corporation for additional lifeboats on the BUNKER HILL, MASSACHUSETTS, and OLD COLONY.

When the COMMONWEALTH was new and the night steamers were at the height of their popularity, travelers would come aboard if they could get a foothold on the gangway and face sitting up all night. Indication of the effect of the automobile and improved railroad service in the 1930s[11] was the reduction in 1934 of lifeboat equipment on the COMMONWEALTH and PRISCILLA to provide for 630 and 605 passengers respectively.

Reference was made to the "enviable safety record" of the Fall River Line. It has been published that the Line never lost a passenger. Officially, the Fall River Line stated again and again that in its ninety years of service the life of but one passenger was lost through accident (PLYMOUTH-CITY OF TAUNTON collision, March 20, 1903). J. Howland Gardner, whose entire business career was with the Fall River Line and whose father was an official before him; Frank J. Wall, Albert F. Haas, and all responsible officials stood by the "one passenger lost" figure. This author's years of research substantiated the assertion. However a recent expression of doubt, twenty years after the Line closed, caused the author to make an extensive restudy of the loss of life at the time of the explosion on the EMPIRE STATE, July 26, 1856.[12] It appears that some of those who died as a result of that blast, previously identified as crew members, were actually passengers; the number may have been as many as nine. Even so, the loss of but ten passengers, in just two fatal accidents during ninety years of all-year-round operation through hazardous waters, is close to perfection in transportation.

This chapter began with the prediction by Louis D. Brandeis that Morse's HARVARD and YALE "would fly the New Haven's flag." Charles S. Mellen stated he "never knew" if the

[11] The Fall River Line passenger average had diminished to one and one-half persons per stateroom.

[12] *Salts of the Sound,* op. cit., p. 61.

New Haven had acquired the two Metropolitan Line steamers. The fact remains that when the HARVARD and YALE suddenly disappeared from the Atlantic coast they were replaced on the New York-Boston run by the New Haven's BUNKER HILL and MASSACHUSETTS. This sentence from the *Nautical Gazette* of June 24, 1915, is illuminating: "It is reported in shipping circles that the *New Haven Railroad has arranged to return the* HARVARD and YALE to Charles W. Morse, from whose control they *were wrested* several years ago."

Did Charles Sanger Mellen have anything to do with the eviction of the HARVARD and YALE? What's your verdict?

CHAPTER SEVEN

Commonwealth Wounds a Battlewagon

Three of the 1907 nautical royalty were almost wiped out on the same July morning five years later! During one of the thickest fogs on record, the COMMONWEALTH, BUNKER HILL, and MASSACHUSETTS, within fifteen miles of each other, had serious collisions. The BUNKER HILL and her sister, the MASSACHUETTS, crashed head-on off diabolical Point Judith. The COMMONWEALTH met an inactive hulk of iron and steel in Newport harbor. The smashup involving the COMMONWEALTH brought legal action by and against the federal government which dragged in the courts for years.

At one-thirty, on the morning of July 7, 1912, off Point Judith, the normally swiftly charging MASSACHUSETTS, commanded by Captain Harold L. Colbeth, poked her prow cautiously through dense vapor. With some three hundred slumbering passengers aboard, she was westbound to New York. Colbeth heard the hoarse whistle of the BUNKER HILL, en route to Boston, in close proximity, and moved the engine room telegraph to "stop." The BUNKER HILL, also moving dead slow because of the nearness of her sister ship, unexpectedly came drifting out of the murk and met the MASSACHUSETTS almost head on. The stout bow of the MASSACHUSETTS bent inward as it pierced a hole in the BUNKER HILL. The ripping and tearing caused great excitement on both liners. Exceptional discipline prevailed and panic was halted. A rudely awakened passenger in BUNKER HILL's room 216, motivated by some sixth sense, had a narrow escape. Leaping from his berth and poking his head out of the stateroom window, he fell back into the corridor in terror as the lofty bow of the MASSACHUSETTS seemed to be seeking him out. The chief engineer's room on the BUNKER HILL was laid open and the ship's barber was forced to flee for his life as jagged splinters, shaving mugs, and hair tonic crashed about him. Exchange of wireless messages between the damaged steamers indicated that both could proceed. The BUNKER HILL arrived in Boston three hours behind schedule, of itself an item of news. Being the more seriously damaged, she was immediately replaced by the OLD COLONY, which later filled in for the MASSACHUSETTS when that ship retired temporarily to have her injured snout straightened.

At 5:05 P.M., in clear weather, on July 6, the big battleship NEW HAMPSHIRE, in company with other capital ships of the North Atlantic Fleet scheduled for maneuvers off Martha's Vineyard, dropped her hooks off Bishop's Rock, Newport. Four hours later, if Captain George E. Rowland, of the westbound PRISCILLA, circling into Newport from Fall River, observed anything unusual about the position of the anchored NEW HAMPSHIRE, he failed to mention it at Long Wharf or by wireless to Captain William B. Appleby of the eastbound COMMONWEALTH. Later in the evening a thick fog set in and the bells of the anchored men-of-war clanged incessantly.

At 3:55 A.M. (July 7), the passenger steamer PLYMOUTH, on the Providence Line,[1] in command of Captain Milton I. Brightman, threaded her way through the murk and the clanging bells denoting the North Atlantic Fleet at rest.

Suddenly an echo of the PLYMOUTH's own whistle bounced back into her pilothouse. The PLYMOUTH was on her course; Brightman and his officers heard no bell or horn, but undeniably a menacing obstruction lay in the channel dead ahead. There was no time for debate, the PLYMOUTH sheered to port and madly reversed. Having averted collision with an anchored battleship by the narrowest of margins, the PLYMOUTH proceeded slowly to Rhode Island's capital city. For some un-

[1] Prior to 1918 the Fall River "winter steamers" operated New York to Providence in summer.

accountable reason Brightman sent no wireless message of warning to Captain Appleby of his company's costly flagship COMMONWEALTH, then berthed at Newport's Long Wharf and soon to follow the identical course up the bay.

Because it was a strict requirement of the Fall River Line that all commanders radio information concerning potential hazards such as ships anchored near the fairway, Captain Brightman's lapse caused much tongue wagging. Did Brightman surmise that the PRISCILLA had already warned the COMMONWEALTH? Did he figure that if his PLYMOUTH could avoid a hit so could the COMMONWEALTH? Was there some doubt in his mind that the PLYMOUTH was on her true course and the less he said about a near collision the better? Could an element of professional jealousy have been a factor? Brightman had come up through the ranks on the Fall River Line; Appleby, originally a Stonington Line skipper, had come into the "family" when the New Haven Railroad consolidated the Sound lines. The official explanation for Brightman's failure was never revealed.

The COMMONWEALTH, with 1100 passengers aboard, rounded Newport's Fort Adams into a busy harbor blanketed by fog. Powerful signals from Newport's four lighthouses, the siren on Long Wharf, and clanging bells on scores of anchored battleships filled the air with dissonance, reassuring to mariners, annoying to landlubbers. The big steamer eased up to Long Wharf and about one hundred passengers disembarked[2] as the deck hands began trundling off freight. The liner cast off for Fall River at 4:13 A.M., to plunge within minutes into one of the most dramatic experiences of her career. Her speed to Gull Rocks was eight knots; there, Appleby gave the order for the normal fog speed of eighteen revolutions (approximately thirteen knots).

At about 4:20 A.M., Lieutenant Harry Campbell, officer of

[2] Most Newport passengers continued to Fall River and came back by train.

the deck on the NEW HAMPSHIRE, heard the whistle of a steamer approaching from Newport. Remembering the narrowly averted collision with the PLYMOUTH, he instructed the sailor at the warship's fog bell to ring it continuously. Four minutes later the worried officer sighted the murk-dimmed lights of a big ship bearing down on the helpless NEW HAMPSHIRE. Knowing that a crash was inevitable, Campbell sounded collision quarters and closed the warship's watertight doors.

The COMMONWEALTH had run her time to reach the turning point where she changed course to head up the bay. First Pilot Senior Grade Daniel Grinnell gave the order to put the COMMONWEALTH on NE×N¼N; the steamer started to swing when her stentorian whistle almost rattled the pilothouse windows as it was deflected back by some massive object directly ahead. At practically the same instant the bow watchman, immediately below the pilothouse,[3] Captain Appleby and Pilot Grinnell, within the circular nerve center above, saw the vague outline of a ship only a few yards away. The engine room gong clanged "Full speed astern," but it was far too late. With her giant paddles banging in reverse, the COMMONWEALTH struck the other vessel and then quivered like a leaf in an autumn gale. Passengers, sleeping fitfully because of the blaring fog whistles, were tumbled from their beds as stateroom equipment was sent flying and crockery crashed from the steamer's pantry shelves. Third Assistant Engineer Herbert W. Alfenburg, after springing to the throttle in response to the frantic signal from the pilothouse, felt as if the ponderous engine was being shaken loose as sounds of tortured metal rang in his ears. "My God," he yelled, "we must have hit the Rock of Gibraltar!" First Pilot Junior Grade Frank H. Avery,[4] off duty and free of direct responsibility, came awake in a second. His first thought was that the liner had run through the dock at Newport. He peered out into the fog as a negro porter rushed by. "What's

[3] Sixty feet from her stem.

[4] Avery was captain on COMMONWEALTH's final voyage, July 1937.

the trouble?" called the navigator, to be met with a most edifying statement, "Captain, ah thinks we've hit something, suh."

The "something" was a big battleship, identity unknown to Captain Appleby at the moment of impact. Appleby gave immediate orders to Wireless Operator Whitehead to send an S O S, and by direct phones from the pilothouse to Chief Engineer John V. Sheldon to check the damage and to Chief Steward John Sullivan to calm the passengers. Scores of distraught travelers in night attire rushed to the liner's damp decks. They were assured that the steamer was in Newport harbor and that there was no immediate danger. Sounds of the crash, followed by the S O S, caused great excitement among the naval units. On several battleships preparations were made to lower boats to come to the aid of the COMMONWEALTH, feared sinking. A wireless message from Captain James H. Oliver, of the victimized U.S.S. NEW HAMPSHIRE, snapped through the fog to the motionless COMMONWEALTH, "Do you need help?" Reports from the mates and engineers convinced Appleby that, while the COMMONWEALTH had a big hole in her starboard side and her bow plates below the waterline were crumpled by the warship's heavy armor plate, she was in no danger of foundering. Appleby decided to turn back to Long Wharf.

Hasty examination indicated that the war vessel had sustained serious damage. The COMMONWEALTH had rammed the NEW HAMPSHIRE's stern at a point about eight feet to starboard of centerline. The battleship's plating above the armor belt was sheared for a distance of about twenty-four feet. Captain Oliver's cabin was a shambles; one officer on the warship had been injured. When the COMMONWEALTH limped back to Long Wharf the letters "New Hampshire" were inversely imprinted on her port bow. The liner, in turn, had left great splotches of white paint on the warship's grey stern. Significantly, the battleship, below the armor belt, showed little evidence of a blow; the COMMONWEALTH's bow below the waterline was mangled.

There were some interesting coincidences involving the two vessels which tangled in the Newport fog. Their actual dimensions were almost identical, although, of course, the tonnage of the warship was much greater.[5] The NEW HAMPSHIRE was 454 feet long, 76 feet beam. The COMMONWEALTH was 456 feet long, 95 feet beam. Both ships when new made the headlines. COMMONWEALTH sailed on her first trip on July 1, 1908. Three days later the recently commissioned battleship NEW HAMPSHIRE, in command of Captain Cameron McRae Winslow, arrived at New York with the world's record for long steaming at high speed to her credit. Coming from Colon, near the Atlantic end of the Panama Canal, she averaged fifteen knots for the distance of 1980 knots.

Winslow, former naval aide to President Theodore Roosevelt, had been placed in command of the U.S.S. NEW HAMPSHIRE on March 28, 1908. As Roosevelt's naval aide he had commanded the presidential yacht MAYFLOWER, and in July 1905 had taken the plenipotentiaries of Russia and Japan to the President's famous home, Sagamore Hill, Oyster Bay. At the time of the 1912 collision the NEW HAMPSHIRE was one of the vessels of the Second Division, Atlantic Fleet. And who was in command of that division and supervised the naval inquiry to fix responsibility for the collision? Rear Admiral Cameron McRae Winslow, whose flagship U.S.S. LOUISIANA, the morning of the accident, was anchored in the fog near the NEW HAMPSHIRE.

Albert Haas has vivid recollections of the Newport Repair Shop's technicians being suddenly summoned to Long Wharf. Later he went out to view the damage to the NEW HAMPSHIRE. A special train took the COMMONWEALTH's passengers to Fall River, there to connect with the trains leaving Fall River Wharf. Gardner and Haas soon determined that the COMMONWEALTH's pumps would control the intake and she left for Hoboken dry dock at 8:25 P.M. The PROVIDENCE took her place

[5] 16,000 tons.

on the Fall River Line; the PURITAN went on the Providence Line. The NEW HAMPSHIRE, after temporary repairs at Newport, reached the Brooklyn Navy Yard on July 14. Her bow rebuilt twelve feet back, the COMMONWEALTH resumed Fall River Line service on August 10.

A lively exchange of "'tis so" and "'taint so" filled the damp air at Newport after the excitement subsided. Captain Appleby expressed his willingness to sign an affidavit that the COMMONWEALTH was on her course and that the hull of the warship had protruded into the steamer channel. Rear Admiral Winslow insisted that the NEW HAMPSHIRE was properly berthed. However, the skipper of a four-masted schooner, arriving in Providence a few hours after the collision, complained that warships had blocked the fairway at Newport. From New York, Fall River Line superintendent, Captain Henry O Nickerson, called attention to letters he had written to the Navy Department, May 4, May 14, June 19, and July 1, pointing out the dangerous anchorage of war vessels at Newport.

At the outset the official blame was placed on the COMMONWEALTH. The New England Steamship Company's rebuttal was emphatic. The naval Court of Inquiry, before which the New England Steamship Company was represented, found that "the naval vessel was anchored in a place where it is customary for such vessels to anchor; no law or regulation prohibited anchorage in this place; there was ample room for vessels of any draught to pass on either side of the NEW HAMPSHIRE; the COMMONWEALTH was proceeding at thirteen knots through heavy fog; her lookout was stationed some seventy feet from the bow and only about five feet from her master and pilot." Subsequently a naval Board of Investigation rendered the verdict, "no blame should be attached to any officer on board the NEW HAMPSHIRE. . . . Responsibility for the accident rests entirely with the officers of the steamship COMMONWEALTH."

Consequently the Navy requested the United States Attorney General to institute a damage suit against the owners of the liner. In turn the New England Steamship Company started proceeding in Congress for a private relief bill. On February 10, 1914, the 63rd Congress passed HR 9848 permitting the steamship company to file a cross libel against the government.

At the trial of the case on October 7, 1915, before Judge Hough, in the Admiralty Court, New York, the New England Steamship Company produced scores of witnesses. One of those who testified was the company's brilliant Captain Edward R. Geer, who was later to become a famous master of the COMMONWEALTH, and as such to be involved in an extraordinary salvage adventure. Geer testified that fog was encountered in the vicinity of Newport on an average of three nights weekly; that vessels entering the east passage of Narragansett Bay (Newport) always steered compass courses even in clear weather; that the location of the NEW HAMPSHIRE at anchor near Bishop's Rock was in the fairway. Veteran Captains Nickerson and the unfortunate Appleby confirmed that the liner was on her course.

To the participants and spectators, Judge Hough appeared to be paying scant attention to the navigators or to the detailed course charts prepared by Albert Haas. At length, the attorney for the Navy, evidently feeling that Judge Hough was bored with it all, arose with an objection. The jurist's response electrified the courtroom and mortified the lawyer. Hough said, "I have been plotting these courses on a chart and they all place the NEW HAMPSHIRE in the middle of the channel." Subsequent comments proved that the judge was no landlubber.

The Navy countered with the claims that the COMMONWEALTH was navigated at too great a speed under the conditions; that she did not slacken in time; that because of the dense fog "she should have sought anchorage." The last suggestion was considered an affront by Fall River Line navigators. For years, sometimes every single night for a fortnight, they had guided the big sidewheelers through pea-soupers, Point Judith to Fall River or Providence without incident. Seek anchorage because of a "little fog at Newport"—skilled mariners like Appleby, Brightman, Geer, Griffin, Rowland, or Whiting? Preposterous!

As to the Navy's contention that the COMMONWEALTH's speed was excessive, Gardner and Haas pointed out that the distance from Long Wharf to Bishop's Rock was about two nautical miles and the COMMONWEALTH could not have been operating at "high speed," especially when hardly warmed up after the stop at Newport.

On February 21, 1916, the United States District Court, Southern District of New York, held both vessels at fault for the collision. The decree confirmed that the COMMONWEALTH had navigated at too great a speed; the NEW HAMPSHIRE had "unnecessarily taken up space in the channel." The Court ordered that each should recover half its damage from the other. Commissioner Edward L. Owen was appointed to adjudicate the conflicting damage claims.

The author was privileged to examine the bulky files compiled by Commissioner Owen. The commissioner disallowed the government's claim for expenses of "a full complement of officers and men aboard the NEW HAMPSHIRE from the time of the collision until arrival at Brooklyn Navy Yard." Among such items, the steamship company had questioned "the need for thirty cooks" on the war vessel during that inactive period. The files indicated that the cost of repairs to the COMMONWEALTH at Tietjen and Lang's dry dock, Hoboken, was $26,005.95; Navy Yard repairs for NEW HAMPSHIRE totaled $24,945.57. By a final decree in the case, the New England Steamship Company recovered $11,848.30.[6] *Actual settlement was not made until* 1925.

[6] Admiralty case 58-1. Decree modified to $10,160.70.

In the period during which the collision claim was in litigation, the COMMONWEALTH had a few minor mishaps. En route to New York on Labor Day night, 1916, with 1500 passengers aboard, her wheel was damaged off New Haven and she did not arrive at Pier 14 until early in the afternoon. The wireless operator almost wore his fingers to the bone sending several hundred messages to the offices of delayed and disgusted businessmen. Late in May 1917 the COMMONWEALTH collided with a car float in swirling Hell Gate but continued her voyage to Pier 14 without assistance. For the Fall River Line flagship the summer season of 1918 was unprecedented. Because of World War I schedule changes necessitated by an anti-submarine net at Newport, coupled with sharply reduced travel for fear of marauding German U-boats, the ten-year-old steamer lay idle at Newport Repair Shops through the normally busy months of June, July, and August. The PRISCILLA and PROVIDENCE were the "summer boats" that year.

John Zeto, now an official of the railroad at New Haven, but in 1925 at J. Howland Gardner's office of the subsidiary New England Steamship Company at Pier 14, New York, recalls the cold shoulder treatment accorded the COMMONWEALTH-NEW HAMPSHIRE damage check. When it was sent to the Accounting Department at New Haven an official there was loath to accept it. According to the perplexed recipient there was no "open account" and the draft should be returned to the government.

Imagine the financially pressed New Haven Railroad even considering spurning good money today!

CHAPTER EIGHT

Enter "Mephistopheles"

In July 1912, when the COMMONWEALTH carved a chunk out of the stern of the Navy's NEW HAMPSHIRE, Morgan and Mellen were navigating in troubled waters. The Commonwealth of Massachusetts and the United States Government, spurred into action by the sensational charges of the relentless Louis D. Brandeis, were raising serious questions as to the future ownership of "Mellen's apartment-house boat," as the COMMONWEALTH was dubbed, together with a score of other Yankee properties which had been sucked in by the Morgan-financed New Haven octopus. According to Brandeis, Mellen's proposal to merge the Boston and Maine Railroad with the New Haven "was the most important question in Massachusetts since the Civil War."

Three Presidents—Theodore Roosevelt, Taft, and Wilson—three United States Attorneys General, the United States Senate, the Interstate Commerce Commission, and several Massachusetts governors became involved in the dramatic downfall of the ambitious New Haven. For almost a decade the leading newspapers of New England were sharply divided concerning the Morgan-Mellen expansionist policies. Mellen was both eulogized and excoriated; even schoolboys came to know who Mellen was. As the tangled affairs of the greedy New Haven were laid bare by the "pitiless publicity" of Brandeis, the New England Navigation Company, owner of the COMMONWEALTH, was cast in the unsavory role of villain. After vainly attempting to unravel the skein of the New Haven's financial crazy quilt, the Interstate Commerce Commission accused the "Morganized" system of being guilty of *"one of the more glaring instances of maladministration in all the history of American railroads."*

Brandeis's far-reaching campaign against the New Haven began in 1907, the year that Morgan-Mellen fought Morse's HARVARD and YALE by launching the COMMONWEALTH, BUNKER HILL, MASSACHUSETTS, and OLD COLONY. Under its Connecticut charter the New Haven assumed almost unlimited privileges. Mellen, contrary to a Bay State law of 1874, had been gobbling up Massachusetts trolley lines. In 1905, the Boston and Maine Railroad petitioned the Massachusetts legislature for permission to do what the New Haven was doing covertly. In June 1906, Governor Curtis Guild, Jr., sent a special message to the lawmakers calling attention to the New Haven's illegal trolley acquisitions. Immediately there was public clamor which did not diminish when it was rumored that the New Haven had secured control of the Boston and Maine. Mellen admitted to Governor Guild that "interests identified with his company" (meaning the New England Navigation Company) had secured a large stock interest in the Boston and Maine. The governor demanded that the legislature act to "prevent control of our Massachusetts railroads passing into the hands of aliens."[1]

General Samuel C. Lawrence and his son, William B. Lawrence, large stockholders in the Boston and Maine, were greatly agitated by the New Haven's control. They retained Brandeis as attorney. Following his established custom in handling litigation of this character, Brandeis declined to accept compensation from the Lawrence family and began his fight against the New Haven as a citizen. Little did he know what a battle it was to be!

One of his first actions to thwart the monopoly, was an anti-merger bill prohibiting direct or indirect control of the Boston and Maine, and demanding disposal of the New

[1] Because of its Connecticut charter, the New Haven was constantly referred to in Massachusetts as a "foreign" corporation.

Haven's already acquired stock not later than April 1, 1908. Brandeis admitted that the proposed legislation was drastic but said he wanted "Mr. Mellen and his counsel to have no doubt as to what it means." On June 11, 1907, Mellen came before the state's Committee on Railroads, the first of his many colorful appearances before federal and state investigating boards. Asked what he thought of the Brandeis bill, his tone dripping with sarcasm, Mellen retorted, "It is not strong enough; I would prohibit anybody from buying the stock; I would put anybody in prison who even discussed the subject." It was his first open clash with the redoubtable Brandeis. The lawyer asked for permission to read a statement to Mellen and to interrogate him. The rail executive stalked out of the committee room with the sharp thrust, "I'll read your statement in the newspapers tomorrow morning." Soon it became known that the federal Department of Justice was eyeing the New Haven's acquisition of its competitors.

Brandeis was a fact gatherer. No clue was too trivial for him to follow. The more he poured over the New Haven's reports and tried to fathom its complicated accounting system, especially as to its legion of subsidiaries, the more he became suspicious that all was not well with the supposedly impregnable New Haven. Mellen refused him any cooperation. Brandeis became convinced that the New Haven had not earned its dividend and that Mellen's reports were deliberately misleading.

Late in December 1907, Brandeis exploded his bomb! The astute lawyer published an official-looking seventy-seven page booklet entitled, "Financial Condition of the New York, New Haven and Hartford Railroad and of the Boston and Maine Railroad." It was one of the most daring pamphlets of its kind ever written. Brandeis claimed that in the six years from 1901 to 1907, the New Haven's increase in liabilities was 366%; its gross earnings increased only 38.5%. Brandeis charged that the road had been nearly two million dollars short of earning its 8% dividend. As a result of the pamphlet, the *Boston*

American challenged Mellen to meet Brandeis in debate at Tremont Temple or Faneuil Hall.

In commenting on the suppression of steamship competition, dealt with in our previous chapters, Brandeis wrote, "No competitor was too large to be overcome and none so insignificant as to be tolerated. The present corporation is not strictly a railroad—it is a general transportation, lighting, power, water, and holding company. Prior to the advent of Mellen the road was conservatively managed; once the strongest financial railroad in America, the New Haven is now perilously weak."

How dare a lawyer, inexperienced in accounting or corporation structure suggest that the Gibraltar of financial strength, reputed as stable as the Bank of England, was tottering on the brink of financial disaster! The New Haven was the trust investment of New England.[2] Upon what meat had Brandeis fed? He knew that Pierpont Morgan's millions were available to the New Haven, that financiers William Rockefeller and George F. Baker were on its board, that Charles S. Mellen was one of the luminaries in the railroad world. The New Haven "perilously weak?" Come now, Brandeis, that is bombast, billingsgate, if not downright blasphemy! So the skeptical comments ran.

Before the Brandeis report, the Commission on Commerce and Industry, upon the urging of Governor Guild, had begun an investigation of railroad combinations including steamships and trolleys. The governor suggested that the inquiry be "conducted quietly." It was! Brandeis assailed the investigation, using such words as "stealth" and "secret inquisition." Its picture of the New Haven's financial affairs was at variance with that of the Brandeis booklet. Mellen rejoiced that the "financial condition of the New Haven was no longer a subject of serious doubt."

[2] Of the 189 Massachusetts savings banks, 176 held New Haven securities.

However, Mellen's joy was short-lived! In the midst of the spirited discusssions concerning the Boston and Maine merger, the New Haven sustained a demoralizing defeat. The Massachusetts Supreme Court held that the railroad's trolley holdings were illegal and must be relinquished. Mellen, having been led to believe that everything was "safe," was astounded at the decision.

In April 1908, the Brandeis-inspired Massachusetts Anti-Merger League was formed. Almost immediately it was offset by an organization called the Businessmen's Merger League. From Pittsfield to Provincetown, Brandeis spoke fervently against the evils of monopoly and the New Haven's queer accounting methods. New Haven Vice President Timothy Byrnes, who possessed "a charming personality and facility of speech," was assigned to counter the disturbing Brandeis attacks. The Brandeis-Byrnes debates are well remembered in the Bay State. Volumes could be written about the victories and defeats in Brandeis long but ultimately successful campaign against the New Haven-Boston and Maine merger. Indeed, such a book has been written.[3]

The New Haven management, methods, and mergers became a national issue. In April 1910, Wisconsin's Senator Robert M. LaFollette, on the Senate floor, inveighed against the New Haven for legalistic delays in federal courts, "until the Administration which brings the suit goes out of office and a new Administration is installed." Federal action against the New Haven monopoly had been begun in the Theodore Roosevelt regime by Attorney General Charles J. Bonaparte. (It was said the President was not eager to move against his "friend Mellen" but the Attorney General was insistent.) On March 4, 1909, the Taft administration took over the Department of Justice. To the consternation of Brandeis, on June 24 Attorney General George W. Wickersham dismissed the monopoly suit

[3] *The Fall of a Railroad Empire*, Henry Lee Staples and Alpheus Thomas Mason: Syracuse University Press, 1947.

pending against the New Haven. It was LaFollette's opinion that, because of its steamship holdings, the government had "the strongest case ever presented under the Sherman Anti-trust law." The *Boston American* propounded the leading question, "Who influenced Taft to withdraw the suit?"

Taft was involved in another chapter in the intricate transportation history of New England. Charles W. Morse, convicted of mishandling bank funds, had begun his sentence in Atlanta on January 3, 1910. Mrs. Morse termed the sentence "outrageous" and started a petition to effect his release. It is said that one prayer for pity contained a half million signatures. The President refused to consider any pardon for the erstwhile Ice-Steamship King. The spirit of the vigorous Morse became broken by the White House refusal and his health began to fail. Once again his friends appealed for clemency. For the third time the chief executive was negative. Early in 1912 it was reported that Morse was dying. Taft sanctioned an order releasing Morse from Atlanta to the Army hospital at Hot Springs. At the same time the President ordered a special board of Army doctors sent to the prison to make a careful diagnosis of Morse's condition. By mid-January word came that Morse, then at Fort McPherson under the care of Army doctors, had suffered a "sinking spell" and it would be impossible to move him to Hot Springs. On January 17, a tearful Mrs. Morse came to Washington to plead with Attorney General Wickersham. The next night commutation of the fifteen year sentence of Morse was signed. In commenting on the action Mrs. Morse said, "President Taft's act is one of simple justice. *I have no hope my husband will live more than two months.*"

Neither the financial world nor the federal courts had heard the last of the "dying" Charles Wyman Morse. He became president of the gigantic United States Steamship Company and built shipyards in Connecticut. In 1922 Morse and three of his sons were indicted in Washington, charged with conspiracy to defraud the United States in the sale of ships, but were acquitted after a long jury trial.

Morse outlived his faithful helpmate. Pardoned in January 1912, as a broken man facing a life span of less than a year, Morse died in Bath, Maine, twenty-one years later at the age of seventy-seven.[4]

In January 1910, a Massachusetts legislative commission, familiarly known as the Validation Commission, made its report on the New Haven. Once again, from a body sanctioned by the authority of the state, the railroad received vindication of its financial position, and Brandeis was held up to scorn. The monopoly's friendly *Boston News Bureau* hailed the "magnificent credit of the New Haven." Deriding the three-year-old-Brandeis pamphlet, the newspaper snorted, "This remarkable concoction is practically forgotten. Even its author might now blush to read it. . . . In 1907 Brandeis said, 'A large reduction in dividends is inevitable.' Three years have passed and dividends have been steadily maintained. Who says insolvency?" The "Mellen-ium" for New England seemed near. But the dramatic fall of Mellen was even then on the horizon.

The first chink in the Morgan-Mellen empire appeared early in 1911. A "recession" brought reduced traffic; the Boston and Maine (New Haven controlled) was especially hard hit. The B & M dividend was cut to 4%, which did its stock market standing no good. New Haven stock also declined. Rumors hinted a coming reduction in the New Haven dividend. Mellen nailed the rumor as "the vaporings of a disordered mind."

Stockholders and some newspapers evidenced alarm; Mellen, as ever, was reassuring. There was no need for concern; naturally, some stock fluctuation was to be expected during a period of "unification and rejuvenation." Drastic reduction of operating expenses was ordered. Serious delays, and worst of all, a series of disastrous wrecks occurred. From June 1911

[4] Suffered a series of strokes in 1926; died January 12, 1933.

to November 1912, twenty-eight were killed and nearly two hundred injured in New Haven accidents.[5] Fearful passengers and discontented shippers became vociferous. Public antagonism against the New Haven, lulled for a time, steadily mounted. A torrent of complaints flooded the Interstate Commerce Commission at Washington. Early in 1913 Commissioner Charles A. Prouty came to Boston to investigate the New Haven's finances, traffic, and service. That blew the lid off!

Even the Interstate Commerce Commission's expert accounting sleuths were stymied when they opened the New Haven's rag bag of railroads, trolleys, steamships, electric light companies, contracting firms, newspapers, hotels, stone quarries, including even a button company. They found that the road was crushed under a staggering load of debentures, watered stock, first, second and consolidated mortgages, notes, and refunding certificates. It appeared that "control" of the New Haven was practically vested in the subsidiary New England Navigation Company. Maybe this lawyer Brandeis knew what he was talking about after all!

Even before Commissioner Prouty arrived on the scene, the New England and New York press sharpened their attack on the New Haven. The *Boston American* in a scathing editorial largely absolved Mellen, placing the blame for the New Haven's ills on J. Pierpont Morgan. The New Haven's tragic wrecks continued, the headlines screamed, the editorials denounced, and the public clamored for strict accountability.

Well, it was all the fault of the "professional agitator," Brandeis! Even two United States senators, friendly to the New Haven, said so. Antiquated equipment, poor roadbeds, demoralized service, engineers who ran hell-bent past danger signals, were strangely forgotten in the railroad's zeal to hang every adverse event on Brandeis.

Morgan entered the fray publicly. Just before Christmas,

[5] Contrast this with the almost flawless ninety-year safety record of the Fall River Line.

1912, advertisements signed by Morgan and Mellen appeared. Mellen charged that Brandeis had inflamed the public by "vicious, cruel attacks on me personally . . . has denounced the management with false and distorted figures . . . has cited accidents, still beyond the reach of human invention, to frighten the public." The New Haven's "megaphone," the *Boston News Bureau,* dubbed Brandeis "the *Mephistopheles* of the New England railroad situation."

For several months Morgan's business associates had seen the financier declining in health. On January 7, 1913, on orders from his doctor, he sailed for Egypt. Three days before his departure he executed his will and left a sealed envelope concerning his funeral service with the rector of his beloved St. George's Church. In March it was reported from Naples that he was on a strict diet, unable to receive visitors, and that his physician was "endeavoring to reduce the number of his daily cigars." On March 31, the overlord of Wall Street died in Rome at the age of seventy-five. His body was transported to Hartford, over his "favorite New Haven Railroad," April 14, only a week before the Interstate Commerce Commission inquiry was to begin in Boston. Mellen was left to fend for himself against "Mephistopheles!"

When Morgan's will was made public, the evangelistic fervor of its opening paragraph[6] astounded most of the nation. It read:

> "I commit my soul into the hands of my Saviour, in full confidence that having redeemed it and washed it in His precious blood He will present it faultless before my Heavenly Father; and I entreat my children to maintain and defend, at all hazard and at any cost of personal sacrifice, the blessed doctrine of the complete atonement for sin through the blood of Jesus Christ once offered, and through that alone."

[6] In 1958 a plaque with these words was erected in a Lutheran chapel, once the Morgan home, Madison Avenue, New York.

On March 6, in a hearing before the Boston Chamber of Commerce, Brandeis demanded the dissolution of the Boston and Maine and the New Haven. He replied to the Morgan-Mellen advertisements by ridiculing the charges that "the knockers" had brought about the reduction in market values of the two railroads or caused the recurring accidents on the New Haven. According to the lawyer, "the order of railroad financing is to look after operating expenses, then fixed charges, and last of all dividends. The New Haven has reversed the order. Mellen is obsessed with the idea that two and two make five."

The eyes of all New England were on the Federal Building, Boston, when Commissioner Prouty began the Interstate Commerce Commission hearings on April 22. Probably not even Brandeis expected the Pandora's box which resulted from the revelations. Prouty himself put the railroad on the defensive at the outset with the cheerless announcement that the commission's examiners found the railroad's juggling of accounts so entangled as to defy investigation. The New Haven's Vice President E. G. Buckland requested that the hearings be private; Prouty tersely refused.

The New Haven's steamships came sailing into the hearing room almost immediately. Examiner David Brown, after searching for months, was unable to explain how Mellen made a sizeable profit in a nine-day transfer of stock from the New Haven to the New England Navigation Company; from the Navigation Company to Mellen; from Mellen back to the Navigation Company; thence from the Navigation Company to the New Haven. Inquiry was made concerning the sale for junk, at a paltry $44,000, of the steamers CONNECTICUT and RHODE ISLAND, costing well over a million dollars when new, and used a few years before by the New Haven to drive the Enterprise and Joy lines from the Sound. The Commission was also inquisitive about a 1912 "dividend" of $2,252,500 received from the New England Navigation Company, which at the time had only $192,471.61 on hand. What were the $36,000

Boy on COMMONWEALTH watches coaling

Electric mules rumble freight aboard

"Let her go," orders the Captain (center)

Casting off from Pier 14, North River

Steaming smartly up the East River

Captain Strickland greets diners

"A LITTLE VOYAGE OF ENCHANTMENT"

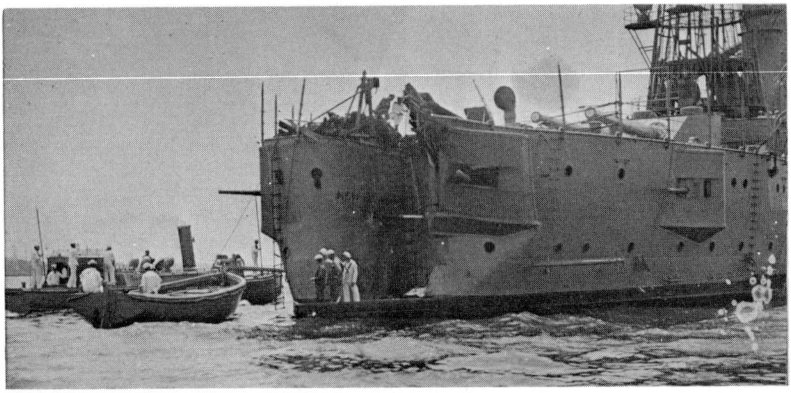

In fog at Newport, 1912, Comonwealth staves in stern of anchored U.S.S New Hampshire

Left: Mangled liner at Newport
Right: Dry dock view of under-water damage

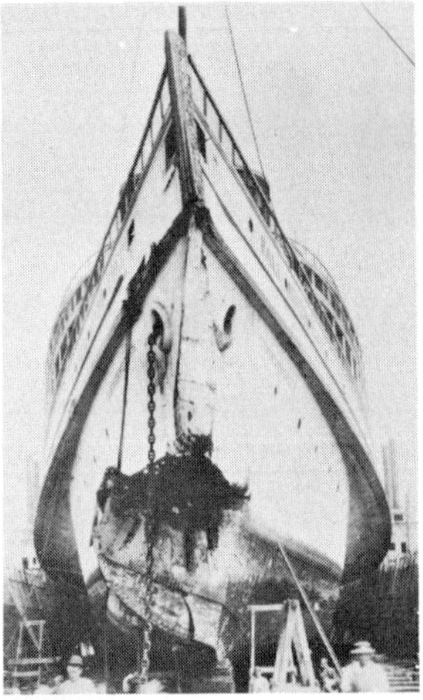

In same spot, Newport Shops, where she burned in 1906, Plymouth caught fire from blazing gasoline welder, Nov. 1919

Eastern proudly announces scenic cut-off

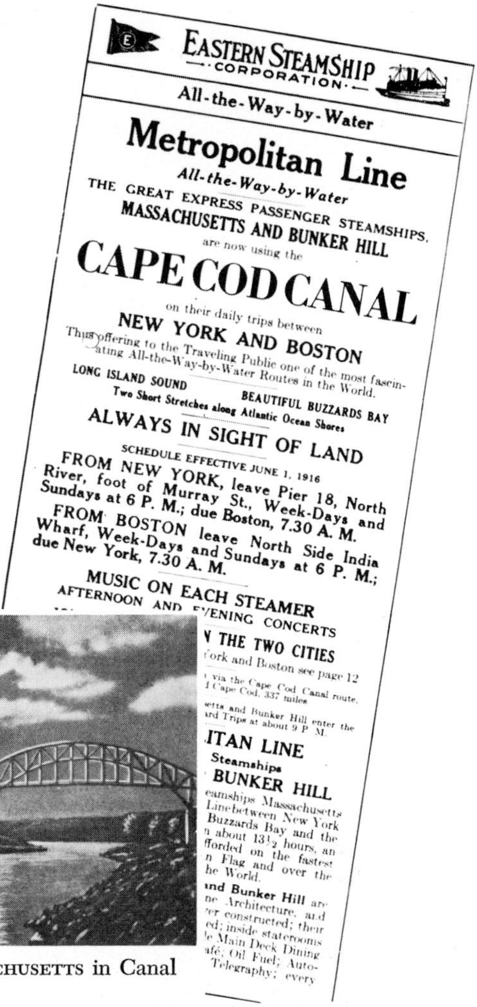

Moonlight view of express liner MASSACHUSETTS in Canal

Skeptics silenced! Fall River's wide PRISCILLA made two Canal trips, June 1937

Top: Eastern's majestic NEW YORK. Right: On maiden voyage, 1924, she smashed Erie ferry ARLINGTON. Below: NEW YORK's attractive Dining Room

Boston's midnight crash with tanker! Ballroom gaiety becomes panic!

Heroes of Boston-Swift Arrow Crash

Wireless Operator E. Walter

Capt. F. M. Hamlen

Chief Engineer P. C. Brooks

Dramatic rescue! Above: Sinking Boston, lashed to side of Commonwealth, reaches Newport. Left: Commonwealth lands survivors. Some of Boston's kitchen crew on upper deck

Form 1204

CLASS OF SERVICE	SYMBOL
Telegram	
Day Letter	Blue
Night Message	Nite
Night Letter	N L

If none of these three symbols appears after the check (number of words) this is a telegram. Otherwise its character is indicated by the symbol appearing after the check.

WESTERN UNION TELEGRAM

NEWCOMB CARLTON, PRESIDENT — GEORGE W. E. ATKINS, FIRST VICE-PRESIDENT

RECEIVED AT US - PIER 14, N.R. N.Y July 31,1924.

MA 419 C

Kalispell Mont 31 125 PM

Captain L.H.Geer,
Steamer Commonwealth,
Pier 14, N.R. N.Y.

In addition to the official letter forwarded to you on July 25th by my direction I wish to personally thank you and the crew of your steamer for the splendid work performed by all at the time of the accident to the Eastern Steamship Companys Steamer Boston. Reports received through our underwriters representatives as well as official company records reflect great credit on you as commanding officer and on your well trained crew not only for the high standard of seamanship displayed, but for the prompt unselfish and efficient assistance rendered to those in danger. You and your crew demonstrated in every particular the high standard maintained by the Fall River Line for over three quarters of a century, and is in accordance with the best traditions of the American Merchant Marine.

J.Howland Gardner - Vice President.

415 PM

Top: Wounded BOSTON, Newport. Right: Capt. Geer's extraordinary salvage hailed; a month later Geer was fired by Gardner

BOSTON as training ship, New London, World War II. She was later sunk by Nazi sub

COMMONWEALTH at mercy of sea, Pt. Judith, 1925. Rescue ships saw only stacks

Broadside view of disabled liner. Paddle wheel was smashed in roaring gale

After hours of peril Coast Guard tows helpless liner to Newport

Several hundred worried passengers cheer arrival of convoy tug, Newport

Winter quarters, Briggs Wharf, Newport Shops. Naval Torpedo Station in background

COMMONWEALTH saved! In 1928 gale she ripped up 40-ton Briggs Wharf mooring (inset), snapped hawsers and swung toward rocky shore

Huge stack removed, Newport Shops, 1929

Below: Look again—it's COMMONWEALTH! Startling photo snapped during reboilering in 1929

"expenses" of securing a pier in New York which were charged by the Quintard Iron Works as "repairs to steamers?" Fundamentally, under the Sherman Antitrust Act, how was the New Haven permitted to be in the steamship business at all?

An incident just two days after the hearing opened was indicative both of the powerful influence of the New Haven and of its methods. Brandeis had been appearing without fee on behalf of the Boston Fruit and Produce Exchange. He was summarily informed that "public representation on your part for the Exchange be not continued." The next day Brandeis presented himself at the hearing as a "citizen of Massachusetts." The New Haven's Chief Counsel Charles F. Choate, Jr., then announced that he too would like to participate as a "citizen." "I represent the people," said Choate, "the same as my dear brother Brandeis." "But, Mr. Choate," Brandeis inquired, "you have been continuously employed by the New Haven."

"That is not true."

"Or by the New England Navigation Company?"

"That also is not true. When I acted as counsel I did so openly."

Fact-gleaner Brandeis then turned to examiner Brown and asked if any payment had been made to Choate by the New Haven. Thumbing through vouchers, Brown stated, "The New England Navigation Company paid Mr. Choate $13,918.82–$7,032.82 for services to the Navigation Company; the balance for services to the New Haven." In a few days "citizen" Choate appeared as "personal counsel for Mr. Mellen!"

On a May day the Boston hearing was thronged to the doors. Newspaper reporters and photographers fell over each other seeking vantage points. Charles Sanger Mellen had come of his own volition to defend himself! Beaming, confident, distinguished in appearance, the white-mustached Mellen put on an unforgettable show. For three hours, eloquent and sarcastic by turns, he explained, explained, and explained the grandiose schemes of the New Haven and his personal faith in monopoly.

To the astonishment of everybody he blandly admitted that he "knew very little about the New Haven's accounts." Actually, he "explained" practically nothing. How could one man explain the workings of nearly three hundred corporations?[7]

Lovers of the Fall River Line are in for a shock. Mellen completely forgot his "apartment-house boat COMMONWEALTH" and her mature sister PRISCILLA. Attorney Choate droned, "Mr. Mellen, I would like to ask your attention to the steamship properties—" He was interrupted by the glib railroader; "The steamship properties consist of three operating companies. Our New England Steamship Company has lines on Long Island Sound from New York to Bridgeport, New Haven, New London, Providence, New Bedford, and the line from New London to Block Island." In a shocked voice Vice President Buckland prompted, "And New York to Fall River."

"Oh, yes, New York to Fall River, of course," responded the abashed Mellen.

Prouty asked about the New Haven's refusal to sell its steamers to Morse. When Attorney General Bonaparte acted against the New Haven in 1908 there was puzzlement over the fact the governments charges against the railroad did not list acquisition of the steamships. Mellen revealed the reason before the Interstate Commerce Commission. He said that in 1907 he went to Washington to confer with "that great and good man" (President Theodore Roosevelt) who strongly objected to the sale. Roosevelt was opposed to Morse controlling Atlantic coastwise shipping. Mellen said the President gave assurance that "the New Haven need not fear any action against it because of its steamships." Mellen added, "I think we made a big mistake in not selling to Morse," to which Prouty responded, "You probably kept Mr. Morse out of jail as much as six months by not taking his offer."

The Prouty hearings revealed deceptive accounting meth-

[7] In 1911 the New Haven was reported to control 311 subsidiary companies.

ods and extravagance. On May 1 the New Haven stock reached 106, the lowest in forty years. Soon came a reduction of the dividend to six per cent. The worst was yet to come!

Despite the glaring public display of the evils of "Mellenism," the New Haven marshalled "political pressure such as never seen in the State House" to pass a bill giving the railroad the right to acquire some western Massachusetts trolleys at a cost of some five million dollars. Governor Foss's veto was fruitless.

On July 9 the Interstate Commerce Commission rendered its report, condemning the policies and methods of the monopoly. On the day the report was issued Mellen resigned as president of the Boston and Maine and the Maine Central railroads. The reason cited was that "it was impossible for one man to direct three railroads." It was known that Brandeis had been in conference with the new Wilson administration; there were indications that the Department of Justice was about to move. The New Haven was now discredited; Morgan had passed on; Mellen was castigated by press and public. On July 17 Mellen resigned as president of the New Haven! On December 10 the New Haven passed its dividend for the first time in forty years. A group of Baptist ministers united in a prayer service in Tremont Temple for the "widows and orphans" whose financial future was darkened by the sharp decline in New Haven stock. In January 1914, the United States Senate, acting upon a resolution by Senator Norris, demanded a broader investigation by the Interstate Commerce Commission.

Even the New Haven's severest critics were not prepared for the shocking disclosures at the second and more thorough Interstate Commerce Commission investigation, which began in April 1914. The inquiry was conducted by Governor Folk, of Missouri. Day by day the amazing story of maneuver and manipulation was unfolded by the tenacious Folk. Double prices had been paid for properties, huge sums vouchered to influence public opinion, dummy directors created wholesale, reporters and college professors subsidized to write favorable stories or deliver "scholarly" lectures on the benefits of a unified transportation system. Most mysterious was the munificent sum of $1,200,000 which found its way to a New York police official at the time the New Haven was creating the unprofitable New York, Westchester and Boston Railroad.

Once again the name of the subsidiary New England Navigation Company was kicked around. Noting that the directors of the Navigation Company were practically the same as those of the railroad, Folk asked Mellen, "How could you tell whether you were having a meeting of the board of the New Haven or the Navigation Company?" Sharp-tongued Mellen retorted, "Just the same as I could tell when C. S. Mellen was doing business, or when C. S. Mellen, president, was doing business."

Folk dealt at length on the relationship of the departed Morgan and the resigned Mellen.

"Mr. Mellen, were you Mr. Morgan's man as president of the New Haven?" asked Folk.

"I have been called by the newspapers his office boy."

"Would you say from your experience, whether you were his man or not?"

"I was very proud of his confidence," Mellen replied. "I desired to equip myself to meet his approval. I regarded the statement I was his man as a compliment."

During the same exchange with Folk, Mellen testified, "There were strong men in the New Haven board other than Mr. Morgan. But I do not recall any time when Mr. Morgan was determined, emphatic, or insistent—I recall no case—when Mr. Morgan did not have his way." In a jocular mood Mellen said, "The record of New Haven transactions with the elimination of Mr. Morgan would have been as tame and uneventful, as devoid of interest or incident, as would the record of a herd of cows deprived of the association of a bull." Testily he responded to the prober, "I had no more to do with the financial policy of the New Haven than I had with the editorial policy of *The Boston Post*."

Shortly after his resignation from the New Haven, Mellen said he would be cast in the role of the "goat" for the financial interests which had hired him. He told a reporter, "I intend to go back to Stockbridge and raise goats. The demand for goats is growing."

This is in sharp disagreement with the position of Herbert L. Satterlee, Morgan's son-in-law. In his full-length literary portrait of the great financier,[8] Satterlee denied that Mr. Morgan had "dictated the policies of the New Haven" and commented on Mellen's "hidden transactions." Satterlee wrote, "With the searching Interstate Commerce Commission investigation of the New Haven, Mr. Mellen proved disloyal to Mr. Morgan and shifted the blame."

The blistering report of the Commission was issued July 14, 1914. It rang with such descriptives as "financial joy riding," "sham methods," "reckless and profligate transactions," "manipulation of securities back and forth" and stressed the dominance of Morgan and Mellen. The report paid its respects to "ornamental directors with childlike faith in the man at the head."

Brandeis's efforts to get action by the federal Department of Justice finally came to a head. Wilson's Attorney General James C. McReynolds[9] seemed no more aggressive in the matter than had his predecessor Wickersham. Brandeis's crusading and the daily tidbits for the sensationalists served up at the Interstate Commerce Commission hearing had so aroused public opinion that McReynolds was forced to act.

Howard Elliott, new president of the system, was bluntly informed that the New Haven must relinquish its control of the Boston and Maine, the trolleys, and the steamships. If agreement could not be reached, proceedings under the Sherman Act would begin. At first, some of the New Haven directors were belligerent, calling the conditions imposed "outrageous and unfair," and indicating that they were eager for a govern-

[8] *J. Pierpont Morgan, An Intimate Portrait,* Herbert L. Satterlee: The Macmillan Company, New York, 1939.

[9] Appointed to Supreme Court in 1914.

ment suit. However, the New Haven's stock had dropped to 59⅛, lowest in the history of the road, and the White House made plain its intention to force dissolution. Consequently, agreement was consummated with a stipulation that the steamship ownership question be left with the Interstate Commerce Commission.

A "reasonable estimate" of the loss to the New Haven by mismanagement and waste was between sixty and ninety million dollars. In an editorial, July 14, 1914, the *New Haven Register* raised a question propounded by many. "Such a sum," said the newspaper, "is not to be overlooked, even when abstracted from the treasury of so large a railroad as this. Where is the money? Who has it? What is to be done about it?" In November a United States Grand Jury indicted several New Haven directors for "criminal conspiracy" but none was found guilty.[10]

When President Wilson offered the name of Louis Dembitz Brandeis for the Supreme Court a violent controversy arose. The Boston lawyer was called an anarchist, chronic howler, a rebel, and a wrecker of railroads. But surprising approval came from a retired gentlemen in Stockbridge, Massachusetts. Charles S. Mellen said, "Brandeis was always on the opposite side from me but I can see no reason why he should not be confirmed." Senate confirmation, on July 1, 1916, was by a vote of 47 to 22.

[10] Six were acquitted; disagreement over five.

CHAPTER NINE

Two Canals Vex the New Haven

From the time of Morse's financial collapse until World War I the Metropolitan Line and the closely related Eastern Steamship Corporation were involved in litigation in the courts of Maine, Massachusetts, Connecticut, New York, New Jersey, and California. Shortly after Morse's pardon by President Taft, his sister, Miss Jennie Rodbird Morse, of Bath, Maine, brought suit against the Metropolitan Steamship Company and the Pacific Navigation Company to "compel the return of the HARVARD and YALE to the New York-Boston trade." Five years later an agreement was reached in a New Jersey court quashing all legal action and allowing the twin flyers to remain on the Pacific.

It will be recalled that the New Haven, through the New England Navigation Company, had a substantial interest in the Maine Steamship Company and the Eastern Steamship Corporation. Under the terms of the "dissolution decree," United States District Court, Southern District, New York, October 17, 1914, the New England Navigation Company was directed to sell 15,000 shares of preferred, 20,000 shares of common stock and bonds to the par value of $2,500,000 in the Eastern Steamship Corporation. The New Haven and the Navigation Company were enjoined from voting upon any capital stock of the Eastern "at any meeting or for any purpose." The practical effect was to make the Eastern a direct competitor of the New Haven and its Navigation Company's Fall River Line.

Theodore Roosevelt's "big ditch," far removed from New England, also threatened the continuance of the New Haven's steamers. In April 1912, Congress passed the Panama Canal Act,[1] which made it unlawful for any railroad to own or operate a common carrier by water. Intended to apply to ships using the Panama Canal, legal lights soon revealed that the law could be interpreted to affect water traffic in all sections of the United States. *Marine Journal,* assailing the sponsors of the act as "Bourbon statesmen from the remote interior," said there was "no real demand for such legislation and the sooner it is repealed the better."

Because of the Panama Canal Act, the New Haven in 1916 filed a petition with the Interstate Commerce Commission for permission to continue its Long Island Sound services. The iniquity of the fathers was certainly not visited upon the children, because New England arose almost to a man in defense of the rail-owned ships. At the very moment the "Mellenized" railroad was being bitterly and severely criticized, its subsidiary steamer lines were praised and saluted as "perfectly managed." A New England Railroad Conference, appointed by the several governors in October 1913, urged retention of the Sound steamers by the railroad.

Rail control of the steamers made for ready adjustments to the joy of shippers and travelers. At Mansfield, Massachusetts, freight trains rumbling to the steamer at Providence could be diverted to Fall River Wharf or from the New Bedford Line to the New London Line steamer. A few times in the winter when the seas were running mountain-high at Point Judith, Fall River Line eastbound steamers put in at New London. From the company's wharf there a special train took voyagers without confusion or expense to Providence, Fall River, and Boston. Steamboat connecting trains at Fall River Wharf were "guaranteed connections," thus saving New York-bound travelers grey hairs or palpitations of the heart. The author has a vivid recollection of a Labor Day night when the already crowded steamers PLYMOUTH and COMMONWEALTH

[1] *The Old Fall River Line,* op. cit., p. 138.

patiently simmered at Fall River Wharf for three hours awaiting the arrival of the Nantucket-Martha's Vineyard connecting train from New Bedford.

On July 10, 1918, the Interstate Commerce Commission modified the Panama Canal Act so far as the New Haven was concerned. In approving the railroad's retention of its Sound steamers the decree made a cogent observation. Said the Commission, "It is unquestionable that at this time and probably for a long time to come, *if not permanently,* the public interest will require maximum use of water transportation on the Sound." Ah yes, in 1918 the future service of the Sound steamers was considered permanent!

A canal much nearer home vexed the New Haven about the time the Interstate Commerce Commission voided the restrictions of the Panama Canal Act. As early as 1623, the Plymouth colonists talked about a canal across Cape Cod to permit them easy access with the Dutch at New Amsterdam. In 1776 George Washington dispatched an engineer to check the feasibility of the project. For years there was talk and surveys, followed by much breast-beating but no shovel-wielding. In 1909 a private firm headed by August Belmont began the digging. In view of subsequent developments affecting the COMMONWEALTH and the PRISCILLA it is interesting to note that in 1912, one hundred fifty delegates left a convention in Philadelphia to inspect construction of the Massachusetts canal. The journey was made by Fall River Line and a special train Fall River to Buzzards Bay. Calvin Austin, president of the Eastern Steamship Corporation, fairly bubbled when he saw the ditch, exulting that it would "revolutionize shipping between Boston and New York." The Cape Cod Canal was opened to small craft in 1914 as a toll waterway.[2]

Early in 1916, *Marine Journal* felicitated Captain Jacob W. Miller,[3] Belmont's right-hand man, for engaging Captain Ed-

[2] Taken over by the federal government in 1926.
[3] New Haven's former Sound Lines general manager.

ward R. Geer as superintendent of the Cape Cod Canal, with headquarters at Buzzards Bay. Geer, one of the most distinguished skippers in the annals of Sound steamboating, went to sea as a mere boy and later, in 1890, was employed by the New Haven marine outfit as a quartermaster. Ten years later he was a master, handling the big Sound steamers with exceptional skill. From 1905 to 1910 he was on leave of absence, commanding Standard Oil tycoon Henry H. Roger's yacht KANAWHA. He rejoined the New England Steamship Company in 1910 and was given the speedy round the Cape freighter OLD COLONY.

The Eastern's Metropolitan Line was giving serious consideration to using the Cape Cod Canal as a feature of the tenth season of New York-Boston direct passenger service. In May 1916 both the MASSACHUSETTS and the BUNKER HILL made trial runs through the Canal.

Up to that time the honor of being the heaviest draft vessel to go through was held by Metropolitan's freighter JAMES S. WHITNEY. A few weeks later Geer piloted the swift MASSACHUSETTS through the Canal, inaugurating regular passenger service by that route.

Use of the Canal gave the Metropolitan Line "one of the most fascinating all-the-way-by-water routes in the world" and they lost no time exploiting the advantage. The schedule of their "great, express passenger steamers" was reduced from fifteen to thirteen and one-half hours. Eastbound, the Canal was entered at 3 A.M., but hundreds arose and gathered on the decks, often in scant attire, to watch the steamer wind her way between the narrow sandy banks. By June the Metropolitan's advertising for the first time featured "music on each steamer." In October, when the Metropolitan normally stopped carrying passengers for the winter, Orlando H. Taylor, passenger traffic manager, announced that use of the Canal had met with such "wonderful favor" that the MASSACHUSETTS and BUNKER HILL would continue in service through the winter. The New York-Boston fare would be $3.00; staterooms reduced to $1.00; table d'hôte and à la carte dinners and club breakfasts provided; music by selected artists from Dagett's Boston Orchestra would offer entertainment. The records show that the Metropolitan in 1916 continued passenger service until December 13, the latest date, prior to operation of full winter service a decade later.

Successful nagivation through the confined Canal in the early years was a tribute to the Metropolitan's mariners. The scenic cutoff was winding and narrow (when first built only one hundred feet wide on the bottom, according to Captain Harold L. Colbeth) and a strong tide was normally encountered. Minor groundings were frequent; major accidents rare. One of the latter was suffered by the BELFAST,[4] making the first eastbound trip of the 1919 season. On the morning of April 16, the BELFAST, commanded by Captain Harland W. Robinson, with one hundred fifty passengers, ripped out twenty feet of her forward deck, several staterooms, and part of her pilothouse when she collided with the Sagamore highway bridge. Three passengers were seriously injured. After striking the bridge abutment, the BELFAST swung around and completely blocked the Canal. In 1934 the Canal was widened and deepened at a cost of $30,000,000. It is now 17 miles long, 540 feet wide, and 32 feet deep.

Captain Geer left the Canal's executive post in 1917 and returned to the Fall River Line. In 1922, Captain Appleby suffered a slight stroke on the COMMONWEALTH and Geer surrendered the helm of the PLYMOUTH to Captain Robert M. Robinson and took command of the giantess. Nobody ever handled the mammoth COMMONWEALTH like Geer! Many times, both at Fall River and New York, he docked her without the use of a single berthing line, an incredible achievement. However, two years later the able and highly praised Geer was forced to surrender Fall River's flagship to Captain Robinson,

[4] BELFAST, World War I replacement, later became ARROW, Colonial Line.

as an aftermath to performing one of the greatest feats of navigation and salvage in maritime history!

There were some minor incidents before Geer's spectacular feat. On the morning of May 25, 1923, nearing Hell Gate, the radius rod on a COMMONWEALTH paddlewheel broke and Captain Geer anchored the big craft and radioed for assistance. The municipal steamer RIVERSIDE responded and took off a few of the liner's five hundred passengers whose urgent business required their presence on shore. The COMMONWEALTH was towed to a pier at North Brother's Island and the remaining passengers were removed by tugs. She sailed eastbound on time that night.

The popular liners MASSACHUSETTS and BUNKER HILL became U.S. Navy mine layers in World War I, and the Metropolitan was forced to operate smaller ships via the Canal for several summer seasons. These included the BELFAST and the CAMDEN, from the Eastern's Bangor Line, the NORTH LAND and the CALVIN AUSTIN. Contracts were placed for new sister ships, expected to outdo the HARVARD and YALE, thus causing travelers to forget them as well as the MASSACHUSETTS and BUNKER HILL, not to mention forsaking the rivals COMMONWEALTH and PRISCILLA. The new steamers were modified trans-Atlantic liners, with running water in every one of the 345 staterooms. A score of deluxe rooms had tiled baths and both hot and cold running water.

Because of accidents, the swanky new 402-foot-long liners BOSTON and NEW YORK[5] were in the news at the outset of their service in 1924. The BOSTON made her maiden voyage, New York to Boston on June 3. Some six weeks later, off Point Judith, only her stout construction, the heroism of her wireless operator, Elmer H. Walter, the brawn of the COMMONWEALTH and the skill of Captain Edward R. Geer kept the costly BOSTON from

[5] Designed by Theodore E. Ferris; built by Bethlehem Steel Co., Sparrows Point, Md.

being a short-lived Sound queen like the ill-fated ATLANTIC of 1846.[6]

The NEW YORK climaxed her first revenue trip through the Canal by sending the New York police, photographers, and reporters hastening to Pier 19, North River. She made a "crashing" finish to her maiden voyage from Boston July 7. The author has clear and vivid recollections of that morning; it was his sole experience with "shipwreck." The NEW YORK was due at 8 A.M.[7] and was annoyingly about a half-hour late. Consequently, Captain Harland W. Robinson did not want any further delay in the stream. The Erie Railroad's Chambers Street ferry slip adjoined Pier 19. The ferryboat ARLINGTON, from Jersey City, also eager to avoid any delay, did not slow up, and finally tried to make an end run around the big NEW YORK, with the result that the ferry received a fifteen-foot hole in her starboard side. The lively fifteen minutes terrified some of the ferry passengers, many of whom were New Jersey neighbors of the author.

That July morning the author was all eyes for the NEW YORK. Standing on the ferry's forward deck he noted at once that the new liner had not arrived. Then he spied the proud, glistening, flag-bedecked coastal steamer rounding the Battery from the East River and was exultant because that would mean a close-up view of the publicized craft. A Jersey-bound ferry poked out of the Erie's slip about the time the NEW YORK was off the competing Fall River Line dock at Fulton Street, and the Sound steamer slowed. Possibly Captain Robinson decided he would not defer to a second double-ender, because the NEW YORK quickly resumed speed. Before the ARLINGTON began a frenzied tooting, the author had the first intimation of trouble. An officer on the bridge of the NEW YORK was observed frantically waving the astern signal to Captain Robin-

[6] *Salts of the Sound,* op. cit., p. 99.

[7] Steamer left Boston at 5 P.M.; Fall River boat train at 6 P.M., but Fall River steamer arrived New York 7 A.M.

son, who had gone aft to the liner's docking bridge. By this time Captain Alexander McKeever of the ferry had no real choice; he had to make a run for it. There was a terrific crash and the prow of the NEW YORK unceremoniously splintered the ARLINGTON's decks, siding and men's cabin seats, where scores of commuters had been sitting seconds before. No one was seriously hurt, and in a quarter of an hour the passengers were streaming off the bruised ARLINGTON.[8] Scratches marring her new white paint were the only evidence the NEW YORK bore of the collision.

[8] ARLINGTON ended Erie's ferry service, December 12, 1958.

CHAPTER TEN

Commonwealth Salvages New Luxury Liner

Long Island Sound has its "night to remember." In imagination we shall embark for New York on the brand new BOSTON, leaving that city's India Wharf on the sunny afternoon of Monday, July 21, 1924. Through the eyes of mariners, wireless operators, engineers, and passengers we shall live again the fearful hours off Point Judith.

Some seven hundred were booked for the voyage—businessmen, families, honeymooners, and vacationists—a cross section of America. The liner steamed through calm Massachusetts Bay toward the Cape Cod Canal. Early evening passage through the Canal never failed to be exhilarating to the officers and crew of the BOSTON. There was a camaraderie with the friendly folk whose familiar but nameless faces lined the banks night after night. Wireless Operator Elmer H. Walter always slipped out on deck at the Bourne Bridge because a pretty girl waved and called down, "Hello, Sparks." Autos by the score honked in salute, and Captain Alfred W. Call, in acknowledgment, sent the BOSTON's powerful whistle bouncing around the dunes and the pines.

As the Canal was left astern and passengers crowded into the ballroom and the veranda café, the BOSTON ran into light fog. At Hen and Chickens Lightship, where the liner shaped her course for Point Judith, it became a regular "pea souper." Chief Officer A. C. Morton summoned Captain Call to the bridge.

The faint sound of a horn from a schooner caused the BOSTON to come to a dead stop. A quartermaster, hastening aft, stopped by the door of the radio shack and said to Walter,

"Boy, we just had a close call with that damn schooner. You can't hear their crazy horns until they're right under your bow." A few minutes later a powerful whistle was heard close by. Two blasts from an unseen ship came through the fog; the BOSTON blew three blasts, signifying that she was going full speed astern. Walter, sensing a confusion of whistles, stepped across the deck, grasped the port rail and was startled to see the ruby and emerald running lights of a ship coming right at him, only a few feet away. The BOSTON trembled as her twin screws churned in reverse. There was a terrific crash, a jolting shudder, the ripping and tearing of steel and wood. A black prow knifed into the port side of the passenger ship, about the middle of the boiler room, smashing several staterooms. Walter knew the ship was in real trouble and rushed to the sleeping quarters to awaken Junior Operator Charles E. Sullivan. Having recently been in a collision on a Savannah Line steamer, Sullivan exclaimed, "My God, have I got to go through one again?" The two grabbed their life preservers and raced back to the radio room.

Captain Charles T. Snow, born at Wellfleet, near the tip of the Cape, had gone to sea at an early age. In 1900 he joined the Metropolitan Line. Later, as the intrepid master of the NORTH LAND, New York to Portland, he had many a heated dispute involving "rules of the road" with Captain George E. Rowland of the PRISCILLA. Subsequently, as the port captain of the Eastern, he had carefully studied the BOSTON under construction. Captain Snow knew every inch built into the new Sound steamer. He was aboard the BOSTON on the fateful night.

Snow was preparing to retire when he heard the whistles thundering out their warnings. He sensed that a crash was imminent and raced for the bridge, reaching there just after the collision. Chief Officer Morton was shouting by megaphone to the officers of the other ship, now identified as the tanker SWIFT ARROW, Mexico to Fall River, asking her to stand by to take passengers from the BOSTON. Captain Call, convinced that the BOSTON would go down quickly, had given orders to abandon ship and asked Captain Snow to relay that dread word to the wireless operator. Snow, realizing the danger of sending lifeboats into the dense fog, and noting that the ocean was calm, felt that the BOSTON would stay afloat and that the launching of lifeboats could be delayed. But honoring the code of the sea, Snow knew that Call's order must not be questioned.

Captain Snow burst into the radio room and commanded, "We're hit badly, send out the S O S." He gave the ship's position and hastened below to survey the damage. The rescue of eight hundred fifty persons was in the hands of twenty-three year old Operator Elmer Walter! Walter's fingers flew into action and the alarming plea went out to all ships at sea—"S O S—S O S—S.S. BOSTON rammed and sinking two and one-half miles southeast of Point Judith, Rhode Island—Call, master."

The first response to Walter's call for immediate assistance was from the British ship ORDUNA, bound for England, and too far out in the Atlantic to be of prompt assistance. At that moment something caused Walter to glance up from his all-important key. He had placed his life preserver on a table near the set. A terrified passenger had grabbed it and ran down the deck. Walter completely forgot the peril of the ship and the S O S. Madly he dashed after the thieving passenger. As he snatched his precious life preserver away, the passenger blurted out, "I can't swim." "Neither can I," responded the operator as he tore back to duty. In those awful seconds of "desertion from his post," the instinct of self-preservation had blotted every other thought from Walter's mind. Walter sent Operator Sullivan to the bridge for orders and he brought ominous news from the worried officers there.

Snow was one of several officers reporting from below decks. The mariner found two compartments full as the waters of the Atlantic poured into the gaping hole in the liner's side. Chief Engineer Roy Fox was cutting out the boilers to prevent an explosion. Soon the electric lights went out and there was no steam power for the whistle. On the upper deck, Walter, feverishly sending and receiving messages, shifted to auxiliary power and connected his table light to that source. The whistle having failed, the BOSTON's only effective voice was Walter's sending key!

As Captain Snow hurried along the lower deck after his disconcerting inspection of the awesome damage, he heard a strange sound, almost like the braying of a donkey. He quickly located its source in a secluded corner of the freight deck. One of the steamer's dining room waiters was sound asleep, snoring loudly. Shaken awake by Snow, the astonished darkey was ignorant of the fog, the terrible collision, and that the proud BOSTON seemed doomed!

While snapping out messages of the peril off Point Judith, Walter was conscious of background noises, sobbing, yelling, and general confusion. Sullivan was in and out of the radio room and able to see the frenzied deck activity. He told Walter that half-clad passengers were scrambling into the lifeboats. Sullivan had heard one of the officers tell Captain Call that some passengers were feared killed in wrecked staterooms 40, 42, and 44.

"Here's damn good news to take to the captain," yelled Walter as he typed a message for Sullivan to carry to the bridge. Captain Fred M. Hamlen of the competing Fall River Line's PRISCILLA, also westbound, forty miles ahead, reported that she was turning back at full speed. This was followed by a message from Captain Edward R. Geer, of the eastbound COMMONWEALTH, advising that she was proceeding to the disaster scene. Due to the heavy radio communication, Operator Sloane, of the sister ship NEW YORK, had great difficulty believing that the "unsinkable" BOSTON was in serious difficulty. "What do you mean you're rammed?" was his radio query. When Sloane comprehended that the BOSTON was sinking, the tone of his reply changed instantly. "Proceeding to you at full speed," came Captain Robert H. Allen's message.[1]

[1] Because of fog and fear of running down lifeboats, the NEW YORK did not reach exact spot.

The SWIFT ARROW, with a big hole in her bow, remained close at hand. Radio communication between her and the sinking BOSTON was faulty and broken. Walter and Sullivan arranged a code system by which the tanker answered messages by signals from her whistle. Captain Call learned by this method that only a few of the lifeboats had reached the tanker. He was gravely concerned that the tiny, drifting lifeboats might be run down by the ships speeding to the rescue. Operator Walter received Call's permission to assign a different whistle signal to be used by the PRISCILLA, COMMONWEALTH and NEW YORK, nearest of the answering ships. In this way they could be directly warned when they reached the lifeboat area.

The PRISCILLA, then thirty years old, was the first to reach the wallowing BOSTON. Details of Captain Hamlen's expert navigation and of Chief Engineer Peter C. Brooks "turning the engines as fast as they will go" have been given in the author's *Priscilla of Fall River*.

The BOSTON's bell was the sole audible means of indicating her position. Walter at the radio key and Sullivan on deck listening for the nearing whistles formed a unique but highly important radio-whistle communications system. Just before 2 A.M., PRISCILLA's blasts told of her cautious approach through the fog. After dispatching the warning, "Be careful of small boats on starboard side," Walter practically "navigated" the PRISCILLA to the BOSTON, whose guard rail on her damaged side was now actually touching the ocean waters. Her peril was acute.

Mrs. Wesley F. Besse, whose menfolk were seafarers, was greatly disappointed. Returning to her home in New Jersey on July 21, she sought a stateroom on the new BOSTON. "Sorry, all sold out," was the response. She obtained a reservation on the PRISCILLA, a ship on which she had traveled many times. "Well, I'll have one of those famous PRISCILLA chicken pies for dinner," she mused, attempting to temper her regret at missing a voyage on the heralded new liner. Hours later, as she watched a drama of the sea unfold, Mrs. Besse was grateful that no BOSTON stateroom had been available!

As a frequent Fall River Line traveler, Mrs. Besse was not unduly disturbed by the thick fog encountered by the PRISCILLA on leaving Newport. After retiring, she was aroused by voices, heavy footsteps, and strange noises from above. Clearly, the PRISCILLA was under way, yet the unusual activity persisted. She dressed and went out on deck. To her astonishment the steamer appeared to be traveling at very high speed through the dense fog. Glancing above she observed that the lifeboats were swung out. Scores of concerned travelers were gathering on the damp deck. Inquiry yielded the disquieting news that the speeding PRISCILLA had received an S O S from the BOSTON, sinking off Point Judith.

More and more PRISCILLA passengers came from their staterooms. An officer called for attention, announcing that the steamer would soon reach the disaster scene and asking those willing to share their staterooms with survivors to register their assent. Then, the PRISCILLA was slowing, stopping, and starting again, her whistle blaring continually. Nothing but fog could be seen. Finally the steamer lay to, a few lifeboats came alongside, and the PRISCILLA lowered some of her boats. Soon PRISCILLA passengers saw survivors, some only partially clothed, being brought aboard. They were taken to the dining room for soup and coffee.

Mrs. Besse extended hospitality to a distraught woman from the BOSTON, who was in scanty attire and had lost practically everything because she had sent her clothes to the ship's tailor for pressing. To this survivor, the terrifying experience of going down in a lifeboat, drifting uncertainly in the fog, and hearing unseen steamers bearing down on their tiny craft had been made more acute when the lifeboat filled with water because a plug had not been inserted.

Among the first of the nearly five hundred survivors to reach the security of the PRISCILLA were two persons very much in the limelight. Miss Corliss Palmer, southern belle, winner of a national beauty contest sponsored by the wealthy magazine publisher Eugene V. Brewster, was the first woman to be put in a BOSTON lifeboat. Mr. Brewster and relatives of Miss Palmer were also traveling on the BOSTON and were rescued. Young Boy Scout Paul Hollister proved the value of scouting's motto, "Be prepared." Finding tearful three year old Billy Gramley, clad only in underwear and sandals, Hollister became his buddy and personally placed him in a lifeboat. Next morning at New York the youngsters were widely photographed, as was a rescued bulldog pup. Among the most fortunate aboard the PRISCILLA were Mr. and Mrs. William Lyman and their young son. In BOSTON's stateroom 46 they had slept next door to death and destruction. The SWIFT ARROW's prow had wrecked adjoining cabins 40, 42, and 44, killing their four occupants. The tales of survivors varied. Some reported efficiency and heroism; others claimed confusion and panic aboard the BOSTON. Captain Call was later quoted as saying, "The passengers were the most orderly I have seen under such circumstances."

Two eastbound Fall River Line steamers, COMMONWEALTH and PLYMOUTH, groped through the fog approaching the constricted passage, The Race. Within hours Captains Geer and Robinson were to team up in one of the famous exploits of the sea.

When Captain Geer answered the COMMONWEALTH's pilothouse phone and received the excited wireless operator's startling report of the BOSTON's peril, one wonders if the first words to fall from his lips were his classic, "By God, I'll do it!" Noted for his quick thinking, a picture of decisive action formed in his mind. Geer ordered his operator to radio Captain Call, "Stand by prepared to take our line."

As long as East River mariners live, Edward Geer's, "By God, I'll do it," will be remembered, and the circumstances told and retold. Captain Frank H. Bunce, who began his distinguished career on the Fall River Line and later commanded tankers sailing all over the world, was pilot under Geer on the swift freighter OLD COLONY in the heyday of the Morse-Mellen competition. One afternoon at Boston, Geer got a message from Captain H. O. Nickerson, Superintendent, who sensed a longshoremen's strike brewing at New York. Geer was ordered to get the OLD COLONY into New York *early* the next morning. With a determined chuckle Geer ejaculated, "By God, I'll do it!" The chief engineer was delighted to assist, for it was his contention that the OLD COLONY was faster than her vaunted sisters MASSACHUSETTS and BUNKER HILL. The freighter was "hooked up" the instant she cast off. She fairly flew around Cape Cod and through Long Island Sound. The next morning the OLD COLONY tore down the East River, Geer outdoing Captain Walter Hazard on his best day.[2] A normal Boston-New York voyage of the heavily loaded OLD COLONY averaged eighteen hours; Geer's epoch-making trip was made in thirteen hours, seven minutes! Scores of damage claims to East River barges, tugs, and wharves resulted. (Bunce said that leaving New York in the evening Geer frequently had the OLD COLONY "hooked up" in the East River with the comment, "The hell with them; it's dark, they can't see who we are; if they complain, I'll deny everything.")

The thrilling race of the PRISCILLA and COMMONWEALTH through thick fog on the night of July 21, 1924, has few parallels in the history of marine disasters. But let Chief Engineer John V. Sheldon of the COMMONWEALTH describe what happened:

> "We had been loafing along at about twenty-one turns because of the fog and practically no freight[3] and there was no need of getting into Newport until 3:30 A.M. When

[2] From Hazard's official record—"Warned for last time about running too fast in the East River."

[3] Motor truck competition. Contrast with September 18, 1908, when she was forced to leave sixteen carloads behind at Fall River.

Captain Geer got the second wireless 'we are sinking,' he ordered me to really go. The PRISCILLA got the message, too. She turned around and headed back. When we came out through The Race we were nearly even. But right in front of us was a tow of barges. We had to stop, while the PRISCILLA was steaming away. When we did get started we began to pick up fast, twenty-three turns, twenty-five turns, and finally twenty-seven turns. The fog was so damn thick you couldn't see a thing. The PRISCILLA got to the BOSTON first. We were close behind. Geer is a real skipper. He swung our ship around and came alongside the BOSTON on her starboard side. She can thank Geer that she remained afloat."

Yes, indeed, Geer was a "real skipper." After narrowly missing one of the drifting lifeboats, whose frightened occupants were taken aboard, the COMMONWEALTH, directed by Operator Walter's radio messages, came inching up to the BOSTON. Only a skeleton crew remained aboard the lightless, lifeless BOSTON. Megaphone messages went back and forth between Captain Geer, Captain Call, and Captain Snow. After what seemed like hours of expert maneuvering, Geer got his giantess directly alongside and lashed the water-logged BOSTON to her side. Geer stationed deckhands with axes at every hawser with life and death orders to chop them away instantly on his signal if the BOSTON started a downward plunge. By then, Navy vessels had arrived from Newport and also put out lines to the damaged steamer. The fog was as thick as ever. Geer, receiving assurance that his own line's PRISCILLA, PROVIDENCE, and PLYMOUTH had picked up the hundreds of survivors, concentrated on getting the BOSTON into Newport.

But at this point, Captain Robert M. Robinson and his PLYMOUTH unexpectedly took the leading role in the dramatic salvage. Two PLYMOUTH officers have vivid recollections of events aboard that rescue ship. Captain Norman L. Strickland, first pilot, senior grade, was on watch with Captain Robert M. Robinson. E. P. Kelly, now an official of the New Haven's Passenger Traffic Department, was purser on the PLYMOUTH.

The PLYMOUTH, eastbound (with some two hundred passengers) was about thirty-five minutes astern of the COMMONWEALTH when the S O S came. Robinson immediately ordered Chief Engineer Herbert A. Scoville to increase PLYMOUTH's speed by two turns. All lifeboats were swung out and boat crews assembled. In less than three hours the PLYMOUTH reached the congested area where the crippled SWIFT ARROW and BOSTON were being attended by the PRISCILLA and COMMONWEALTH. PLYMOUTH put down eight lifeboats, Strickland commanding her boat Number I. The boats went through the fog to the SWIFT ARROW and transferred one hundred thirty shivering persons from the tanker's unsheltered deck. Captain Robinson ordered spare staterooms made available and breakfast served to the rescued without charge.

Robinson, delegating the comfort of survivors to Purser Kelly, faced exacting responsibilities because his PLYMOUTH was to be a "seeing-eye" ship. The COMMONWEALTH had started with her heavy burden but Geer was having trouble handling her. The BOSTON's rudder had been thrown hard left to avoid the collision. In the confusion, its position had not been changed; when the steam power died it had jammed. But that was only part of the difficulty. A wireless message from Geer asked Robinson to check a compass bearing. As Geer suspected, the proximity of the BOSTON's steel had thrown the COMMONWEALTH's compass way off. The resourceful Geer then sent a message to Robinson requesting the PLYMOUTH to proceed through the fog, whistling signals at points where the course changed, the COMMONWEALTH to follow close astern. For all his skill as a navigator, Geer, compassless, was forced to depend on Robinson for the successful conclusion to his venturesome undertaking.

Luckily it was calm off Point Judith. As the convoy (two Navy tugs were on BOSTON's port side) labored slowly toward

Newport, Operator Walter was able to relax for the first time in hours. He found himself ravenously hungry. He breakfasted under the most unusual circumstances. So closely were the BOSTON and the COMMONWEALTH bound together that Walter, a non-swimmer, without the slightest fear of falling into the Atlantic fifty feet below, stepped from his radio room into the beautiful upper deck dining room of the COMMONWEALTH. Almost ten hours after Walter's first S O S had snapped out, the agonizing nightmare was over. The COMMONWEALTH beached the BOSTON on the mud flats of Newport and steamed to Long Wharf, where a great crowd had gathered.

One fully-clothed survivor aboard the PLYMOUTH stood out in particular. Oscar Green, of Brooklyn, returning to New York on his honeymoon, having narrowly missed death, was now beside himself with doubt and grief. He and his bride had occupied a wrecked BOSTON cabin. Green had arisen, dressed completely, shoes to necktie, and gone into the lounge for a drink of water. Then came a terrific concussion. Green was unable to approach his stateroom, now a shambles. Frantic calls to his wife, Rose, remained unanswered. Overruling his protests, BOSTON officers insisted he leave in a lifeboat. Radio messages from the PLYMOUTH to the other three Fall River steamers, which had all the survivors, disclosed no Rose Green among the saved. Overcome by shock, and claiming a back injury, Green was taken to a Fall River hospital. At New York, Mrs. Green's parents, hoping against hope, waited in silent sorrow until every survivor had left the steamers PRISCILLA and PROVIDENCE. Hours later, at Newport, the crushed body of the bride was found in the wrecked stateroom. To this day, Kelly has never understood why a traveler, having retired, would get fully dressed merely for a drink of water which could have been brought to the stateroom by an attendant. An outstanding Bostonian, clad only in pajamas when received on the PLYMOUTH, had had foresight enough to jam his money into his pajama pocket before fleeing. He was whisked to a Fall River clothing store to purchase a new outfit.

One obdurate passenger had refused to leave the foundering BOSTON, and came into Newport on the stricken ship. He was E. L. Dressell, German Chargé d'Affaires at Washington. Pointing to a small trunk he said, "It was too heavy to carry off and I could not leave it." He inferred that he would have gone down with the valuable baggage if necessary.

After twenty-two hours of continuous service, Wireless Operator Walter went to his cabin on the beached BOSTON and fell into deep slumber. Hours later Chief Officer Morton released Walter and Sullivan from duty and they entrained for Boston, a city they had never expected to see again. Subsequently, Walter received a cash award, the RCA medal, and the Marconi Scroll of Honor as recognition for the strategic role he had played in saving the new BOSTON.

Praise for the Fall River Line masters and ship personnel was heard on every hand. Captain Geer's feat was especially lauded. On arrival at Fall River, First Pilot, Junior Grade Thomas Nelson was unstinting in his praise for his superior officer. Nelson claimed that "no other captain could have fastened the big COMMONWEALTH to the helpless, water-filled BOSTON and towed her to Newport." "Even when the sea is smooth," Nelson said, "there is a swell, often not noticed, until you get two big ships rubbing together, one rising, the other falling. It was an immensely difficult thing to accomplish and then make proper headway through heavy fog."

Landsmen joined in the eulogies. Two days after the collision, the *Boston Post* had this to say. "They may knock the New Haven Railroad, call it inefficient and run down, but a great part of the BOSTON's passenger list will take off their hats for life to the New Haven's Fall River Line men. They were the real thing. The Fall River Line lifeboats were handled in masterly fashion. The refugees were given a real welcome on the Fall River Line steamers."

In view of the complete about-face concerning Captain Geer which occurred in two short weeks, the adulation of the Fall River Line management is significant. Vice President J.

Howland Gardner, on vacation in the Far West, was proud of his ship and service. COMMONWEALTH's feat proved that he had builded well. His sixteen-year-old COMMONWEALTH had shown no sign of the tremendous strain imposed on her port side.[4] From Montana, on July 31, he telegraphed Captain Geer in part, "Reports received through our underwriters reflect great credit on you as commanding officer and on your well-trained crew not only for the high standard of seamanship displayed, but for the prompt, unselfish, and efficient assistance rendered to those in danger. You and your crew demonstrated in every particular the high standard maintained by the Fall River Line." A few days earlier, Frank J. Wall, Gardner's assistant, had dispatched to Geer the company's official letter of commendation.

The late Mrs. Clara G. Barrows, Captain Geer's daughter in New London, well remembers how anguish quickly followed adulation. The captain and a nephew had opened a bus line between New London and Hartford. Geer came from Fall River to New London once each week to visit briefly with his family and to handle matters associated with the highway operation. On the next eastbound trip following the salvage Geer came home. He brought newspapers telling of his valor and said to his loved ones that he "ought to get a good sum out of it."

It seems clear that when Geer wirelessed Captain Call, "prepare to take our line," he was adventuring for high stakes. Captain Snow told the author he had been convinced from the beginning that Geer expected salvage but there was no choice if the BOSTON was to live and sail again another day. The Fall River Line had a rigid policy of never seeking or accepting salvage for rescue efforts. Geer knew this. However, he advised Wall of his intention of seeking compensation or salvage from the Eastern Steamship Lines. At the outset, the crew of the COMMONWEALTH joined Geer in his claim. Gardner, an admirer

[4] Rubbed off paint was only evidence of COMMONWEALTH's tremendous burden.

of Captain Geer, peremptorily ordered Geer and his crew to withdraw their action or resign. All except Geer complied. The mariner refused to do either. Then came one of the toughest decisions Gardner ever made. Exactly one month after Geer had beached the BOSTON he was discharged. Captain Robert M. Robinson took his place at COMMONWEALTH's "middle window."

A period of bitter recrimination followed Geer's exploit. It was the contention of the Eastern's insurance underwriters that naval vessels had rendered equal assistance in the towing operation and that the PLYMOUTH had performed an inestimable service. Captain Strickland recalls that sparks flew during one New York hearing at which he testified. Geer and Frank Wall exchanged sharp words. Geer insisted that he had not requested the aid of the PLYMOUTH. But the file of wireless messages between the two steamers proved otherwise. Geer was deeply hurt at his discharge by the New England Steamship Company after thirty-five years of distinguished service. After litigation, Geer received only a fraction of what he had expected.[5]

If a Hall of Fame for famous Long Island Sound mariners was ever established Edward Redding Geer's name would be voted in on the first ballot. In his many years of contact with Long Island Sound executives, captains, engineers, and stewards the author has run across many differences of opinion about ships and personalities. *Never once has there been a hint of dissent concerning Edward Geer's professional ability.* This is particularly significant because there was jealousy on the part of some skippers in the New England fleet when Geer received rapid promotions, often advancing over senior mariners. Captains of competing lines—Allen, Colbeth, and Snow of the Eastern; Cobb and Pendleton of the Colonial—spoke of Geer's seamanship in handling the massive COMMONWEALTH in almost reverential tones. Albert Haas, forty years a Fall

[5] Understood to have been less than $5000.

River Line executive, calls Geer "the best navigator in the modern history of the Line." John Zeto, an associate of Gardner and Wall, described the mariner as "exceedingly capable and forceful, with plenty of guts." Captain Strickland, who sailed under him, gave Geer's rating in one word—"Excellent!" Strickland added, "Ed Geer knew his stuff at all times, under all conditions." Captain Frank Bunce, also a Geer pupil, called him "about the greatest seaman the Sound ever had." Strickland said the 1903 collision between the freighter CITY OF TAUNTON and the PLYMOUTH, off New London, "made Geer, who was Johnny on the spot." That foggy night Geer was first pilot on the PLYMOUTH, under Captain "Danger" Davis. The youthful Geer knew every echo, indentation, tide quirk, reef, and smell within miles of New London. It was he who guided the badly damaged PLYMOUTH into New London. Captain J. W. Miller, superintendent, an Annapolis graduate, was greatly impressed. He recommended Geer to Henry H. Rogers, when the Standard Oil tycoon sought a yacht master. Later Miller made Geer superintendent of the Cape Cod Canal. In 1923, the United States Army Engineers appointed Geer one of a three-man committee to study navigation problems in New York's tricky East River.

Strickland is authority for the surprising statement that Geer's COMMONWEALTH was not the first Fall River Line ship to tow a vessel lashed to her side. Long before the days of wireless, the PURITAN, failing to pass the westbound PRISCILLA near The Race, learned at Newport that the then "largest steamboat in the world" had broken a shaft coming from Fall River. The PURITAN came alongside and towed the PRISCILLA to Newport. Of course, the PRISCILLA was not in sinking condition and the operation was in sheltered Narragansett Bay.

Captain Call, of the BOSTON, had difficulties of a different nature from Geer's as sequel to the midnight collision off Point Judith. The steamboat inspectors at Providence held Call rather than Captain Gomes of the SWIFT ARROW at fault, and suspended his license.[6] In January 1925 General George Uhler, inspector general, Steamboat Inspection Service at Washington, overruled the decision and restored Call's license. Uhler found that "perfect discipline was maintained aboard the BOSTON by Captain Call and his officers under the most difficult circumstances. The lifeboats were swung out and lowered with care and deliberation. It was a most creditable and praiseworthy performance under trying weather conditions." The BOSTON, relieved by the CALVIN AUSTIN, was restored to service September 1, after extended repairs at Hoboken.

New London's tall and handsome harbor master gazed with misty eyes as a great white liner was snugged to a berth at the Coast Guard base early in 1942. The official did not have to glance at the ship's name; he knew her well, possibly better than anyone in the port. Conflicting emotions swept over him as he studied the liner's high bow, many-windowed sides, broad decks, raked masts, and the blue and white insignia on her two stacks. That big white liner marked the triumph and the tragedy of his sixty years as a seafarer! The harbor master, as the master of the COMMONWEALTH eighteen years before, had been credited with performing "one of the outstanding rescues in the annals of coastwise shipping."

That rescued BOSTON, requisitioned by a nation at war to train young men in the ways of the sea, had come to Edward Geer's very doorstep! Harking back to a dreadful night off Point Judith, who can blame Geer if he poignantly ejaculated —"By God, I did it!"

A few months later (September 1942), the BOSTON, saved by Edward Geer in 1924, was sent to the bottom by a Nazi submarine. A year later (August 1943) there was profound grief in New England when Edward Redding Geer passed into eternity.

[6] Tanker owners filed libel for $350,000 against the Eastern; alleged BOSTON traveling at excessive speed in fog.

C H A P T E R   E L E V E N

"Pity the Poor Sailors"

Father knows best—or so he said! "The second the steamer leaves Newport we've got to go right to bed; you might get seasick off Point Judith." That was the undeviating order for the McAdam children, the author and his younger twin brothers. It took the edge off the exciting homeward voyage from grandmother's to New Jersey. Until we approached high school age we were never allowed to see or feel terrible Point Judith.

What an event the nocturnal departure from Newport was! We boys could stand on the gallery deck of the COMMONWEALTH or the PRISCILLA looking far down on dimly lighted Long Wharf as the deckhands, their noisy hand trucks loaded with barrels, boxes, and crates, literally chased each other over the freight gangplank. Occasionally, the steady procession of package freight was interrupted by a truck burdened by a giant swordfish, snared off Block Island mere hours before. The maneuvering to get automobiles aboard was a sight to behold![1] In those pre-World War I days, gasoline was not allowed on passenger ships and the auto tanks were drained bone-dry on the wharf. COMMONWEALTH's ponderous first mate, W. Z. Canedy, with a professional air, eased himself behind the auto's steering wheel; ropes were attached to the vehicle's front axle and a half dozen or so brawny men huffed and puffed the helpless conveyance aboard. If the tide was high, the upward tilt of the gangplank pitted heft against the law of gravity. Finally the resisting autos disappeared into the

[1] Author saw five Rolls Royces owned by Mrs. H. Twombly, Commodore Vanderbilt's kin, leave Newport one night.

ship's capacious freight deck and the freight and passenger gangplanks rumbled back on the wharf. As hundreds on deck and dock called admonitions and farewells back and forth, the big wheels banged in reverse while the bow hawsers plumped into the harbor as Dockmaster Jordon's dog barked furiously. The dark water quickly became bubbling white when the agitated salt protested the disturbance caused by the slowly revolving one-hundred-ton paddle wheels. One reverberating stroke on the engine room gong and the toot of the whistle signalled the termination of our reprieve. A hasty glance at the Elm Street pier and grandmother's Poplar Street home was all that we were permitted. Heavy-footedly we turned from the lure of the deck, the shore lights, and stars to the pair of staterooms; we must be spared the nauseating effect of Point Judith!

Every Fall River Line veteran and regular traveler had his "Point Judith experience." That of Captains Robinson and Strickland in the COMMONWEALTH is recounted in the next chapter. There was one night the PRISCILLA, leaving Newport in what seemed a "normal" gale, met such shrieking winds and heavy seas at Point Judith that she took the beating of her life. The late Chief Engineer William McCready and the head waiter, George Mossop, both of whom sailed through hundreds of stormy nights, told the author that they never expected the PRISCILLA to make it. In humility McCready said, "I never prayed so hard for the engine to keep going; a breakdown or smashed wheel would have done us in."

Captain John S. Blank, III, who frequently served as relief bow watchman on the COMMONWEALTH, reveals a Point Judith gem. One night at Newport the COMMONWEALTH took aboard a large number of boots, freshly graduated from Newport's Naval Training Station. The "sailors," bound for New York, were the pre-commissioning crew of the new cruiser U.S.S. NORTHAMPTON. As they roared over the COMMONWEALTH's gangplank their attitude was convincing evidence that they were "shellbacks" and that COMMONWEALTH's officers and crew were sweet milk sailors. The boots took immediate possession of the big steamer, swaggering through the carpeted passageways, singing chanties, passing loud comments, and ogling the fair sex. Blank recalls that he had to haul one ardent tar from the truck of COMMONWEALTH's after flagstaff on the hurricane deck. The nautical gymnast was demonstrating to skeptical girls how real sailors went aloft.

As the COMMONWEALTH prepared to leave Long Wharf some of the exuberant boots insisted on helping by hauling in the hawsers. Several of them jumped to the dock from the slowly reversing steamer and then leaped back onto the moving guard rail. As the COMMONWEALTH rounded Goat Island and headed for the ocean, the noise of their presence was heard from stem to stern.

But nature soon took over! With a full ebb tide and a fresh southwest wind the COMMONWEALTH hit the awesome stretch between Castle Hill and Brenton's Reef Lightship. The liner staggered a bit as she met the charging seas. Then she began rolling lazily as she glided out past Narragansett Pier to Point Judith. Suddenly she was a quiet and a happy ship. Captain Blank was certain the COMMONWEALTH exuded an air of satisfaction over the results of her tactics. (All true sailors feel that ships have expressive personalities.) The COMMONWEALTH had retaliated for the insults from the embryo sailors, chortling in effect, "pity the poor sailors on a P'nt Judy night like this." Her "salty" passengers were now retching over the rails and in the men's lavatories, while COMMONWEALTH officers, watchmen, and porters smirked. The next morning, seemingly "with a satisfied grin on her gilded prow," COMMONWEALTH proudly backed around Pier 14, North River. Minutes later the crew of the U.S.S. NORTHAMPTON quietly and respectfully marched down the gangplank, "a greater credit to the United States Navy than the night before." COMMONWEALTH had indoctrinated another group of Uncle Sam's sailors; literally she was their shakedown vessel.

Even the members of the "Commonwealth Club" had

their disquieting moments off Point Judith. Few people outside the New Haven Railroad ever heard of that worthy organization. Uncle Sam's Armed Forces have the reputation for being entangled in red tape and made weary with buck passing; they could take lessons from the New Haven Railroad. The inoffensive, financially limited "Commonwealth Club" was responsible for high-level conferences and choked files at the Yellow Building in the Elm City. The author indirectly had something to do with the formation of one of the smallest but most noted organizations within the confines of the New Haven Railroad. In 1925, while employed in the Advertising Department in New Haven, one McAdam persuaded several passenger co-workers on a summer Saturday afternoon to chug to Providence behind an iron horse, hop the bus to Fall River and sail to New York on the COMMONWEALTH. In the party were Henry T. Moorehead, Charles F. Clark, Earl R. Kellogg, Otto Gress, Harry Hall, and Malcolm Scott, most of whom had never seen their company's flagship. Point Judith behaved that night, and the voyage proved so delightful to the neophytes that it was repeated each summer. By 1931 the group had expanded to a dozen males who innocently called themselves the "Commonwealth Club."

"Commonwealth Club?—h'mn—I wonder if it is all right for the boys to use that name. I better check on it," said the vigilant chief clerk after debating the weighty matter for several hours. The intent, history, and scope of the group, as well as its desire to appropriate unto themselves the flagship's name, was transmitted to Walter P. Read, general passenger agent. That was too important a matter for him to decide! The memorandum was respectfully referred to "Hello, hello, hello"[2] Francis C. Coley, the passenger traffic manager, before whom all clerks and stenographers trembled. Coley wrestled with the knotty problem but refused to render a decision. The request went upwards to Vice President Benjamin Campbell. Whether

[2] The energetic official's invariable telephone salutation.

the question was placed before the board of directors deponent knoweth not. In any event, the fifteen were finally officially authorized to adopt the name "Commonwealth Club."

When Albert E. Spette became a full-fledged member he breezily chronicled the annual escapades for posterity. On the third annual outing to Martha's Vineyard the seagoing lads were really put to the test. Concerning the post-midnight events, Spette wrote, "By this time we all piled in our berths. Then the COMMONWEALTH starts giving a demonstration of how she can act up. She begins going up and down and sideways all at once. I ask a deckhand what's what and he says, 'It's only Point Judith; don't worry.' "

There were hundreds of regular Fall River Line travelers to Newport, the Cape, the Islands (eastbound every Friday night, westbound, Sunday) who felt they belonged to a Commonwealth Club. They regarded the COMMONWEALTH and the PRISCILLA as clubs afloat. No swanky Fifth Avenue establishment could provide more regal luxury, good things to eat, or attentive servants than the Fall River ships. Over the years a kinship developed between the "regulars" and the ships personnel. The author knew every COMMONWEALTH skipper except Captain Williamson; the two chief engineers, haughty John V. Sheldon, and courteous John McQueen; the three chief stewards, John J. Sullivan, John Woods, and affable Jack O'Connell.[3] The veteran purser, John Ward, took care of the COMMONWEALTH's business affairs when she first came out. Popular successors were Forrest W. Simmons, George E. Miles, E. J. Flynn, and William Gleason. Head waiters who did much to give COMMONWEALTH's penthouse dining room a distinctive atmosphere were Bob Grump, "Bud" Wilson, and Clarence Haskins.

John V. Sheldon, chief engineer during COMMONWEALTH's first twenty years, except the World War I period when he was loaned to the government to help repair interned German

[3] The author was checker on the PROVIDENCE under O'Connell, 1917.

ships, was an aristocrat in appearance and in possession of this world's goods. John Zeto, assistant to the vice president at Pier 14, recalls that when Sheldon's health noticeably declined, the chief left an old shoe box with Zeto for safe keeping. After Sheldon's death in 1928, Zeto was astonished to find the insecure depository crammed to overflowing with securities, mostly telephone stocks and bonds, many dating from the earliest use of that instrument. Sheldon had casually mentioned that, years before, Alexander Graham Bell, a frequent traveler, had "peddled stock" while voyaging the Sound. According to Zeto, Sheldon's brother received a "fortune" from the ancient shoe box. The late William H. McCready, chief engineer of the PRISCILLA, once told the author that to his subsequent regret he did not "fall for Bell's sales spiel."

Courtesy, dependability, and luxury were not the sole attributes of the Fall River Line. No "regular" ever thought of disaster, no matter how thick the fog or ice, how mountainous the seas, how howling the gales. During her twenty-nine years of service the COMMONWEALTH's lifeboat crews won fame. The author possesses a faded, undated news item clipped in early boyhood, telling of the COMMONWEALTH making a rescue at sea. A man named Foley and his dog were rescued when Captain Appleby was alerted that a drifting barge was displaying a distress signal. The item concludes with these words, "The sea was very choppy but the COMMONWEALTH's crew handled their boat with skill." It will be remembered that survivors of the BOSTON collision in 1924 lauded the Fall River lifeboatmen. All of which points up an incident on the COMMONWEALTH at Pier 14, late in her career. John Zeto is the prideful raconteur. One day a high official of the Steamboat Inspection Service from Washington, without the slightest advance warning of his visit, strode into Mr. Gardner's office and demanded an immediate fire and boat drill. The COMMONWEALTH had been tied up for several hours and only the port watch was on duty. The alarm was sounded and the crew was ordered by Captain Norman L. Strickland to cope with an imaginary blaze and to lower several boats. Zeto, who feared the worst because of the abnormal hour and reduced personnel, was thrilled because the boats were down in a matter of seconds. "We of the office staff were simply amazed at the speed of the operation and the nimble way the crew handled themselves. Our Washington visitor was thoroughly satisfied with the performance and so were we," summed up Zeto. In discussing the event with Captain Strickland, the author was informed, "Fire and boat drills were always held the first day after Sunday we were in Fall River no matter what the weather conditions were. We were thorough; all details were carried out in the old tradition[4] from beginning to end. If a government inspector came aboard unexpectedly we had no fear of him."

Lifeboat drills were not without their risk to the crews. During a boat drill on the City of Lowell at New Bedford, summer of 1920, screams suddenly rent the air and the fearful cry, "Man overboard," rang out. Edward Haskins, Captain "Bob" Robinson's waiter, had missed his footing and plunged into the harbor. Without a second's delay, Norman Strickland, then first pilot, dove off the Lowell's top deck, fully clothed, and rescued the drowning Haskins, who was rushed to a hospital. The exhausted Strickland was given a good shot of brandy by Captain Robinson and in no time was again on deck. It was all in the day's work.

My esteemed friend Raymond N. Lee, the youngest freight clerk ever to serve on the Commonwealth, once failed to keep his weekly New York luncheon date with the author. Hours later it was learned that during boat drill on the Providence at Fall River Wharf the morning before, he had slipped on the icy boat deck and been hurled thirty feet to the dock below. Fortunately Ray's injuries were not too serious. Incidentally, our long and intimate friendship resulted from association on

[4] Strickland had served under Capt. Geo. E. Rowland, a stickler for "perfect" lifeboat drills.

that same PROVIDENCE in 1917. The author was dining room checker and Lee, the telephone operator.

Although twenty years have elapsed since the COMMONWEALTH made her final voyage, many nights on her are as vivid in the author's mind as events which occurred yesterday. Of the scores and scores of COMMONWEALTH passages, five in particular stand out. First of these is the night prior to World War I, out of Newport, when Captain Appleby allowed a lad to be in the pilothouse and to blow the whistle. Years later (November 1926), the sad journey home to New Jersey from my father's funeral rites at Newport is indelible in memory. That night the temperature suddenly dropped to zero and a strong wind developed. COMMONWEALTH's exposed, upper-deck, many-windowed dining room simply could not be adequately heated under such conditions. My friend Charlie Clark and I were forced to don our overcoats while indulging in a late snack. The most beautiful of all the treasured nights on the Fall River Line was on the giantess on Labor Day, 1927, when my fiancée and my mother sailed with me. We steamed from Newport to Point Judith on a veritable golden seaway—a broad path of brilliant light from a full moon. Added to the night's splendor was a rich contralto voice coming from the forward deck.[5] Mrs. McAdam and the author have lived over and over again the two glorious nights and a full day on the Atlantic when the COMMONWEALTH took us to the first International Yacht Race off Newport, September 1930. This was Sir Thomas Lipton's final attempt to gain America's Cup. The Line simply outdid itself in the meals served the hundreds of yacht race guests. There was great excitement coming into Newport the second time that historic Saturday morning. (The COMMONWEALTH completed her regular overnight voyage, New York to Fall River, and then sailed back to Newport and the race off Brenton's Reef Lightship.) Never had Newport harbor been so crowded. As we slowly rounded the Torpedo

[5] The *Old Fall River Line*, op. cit., p. 93.

Station I did not see how Captain "Bob" Robinson could ever weave the big liner through the maze of spectator craft of every class and size. Ominously we bore down on a small yacht; a quartermaster rushed out of the pilothouse and hastened aft; COMMONWEALTH pounded in reverse; the second mate peered anxiously over the rail and shouted something up to Captain Robinson. "Let go the anchor," came his order, but too late. The mast of the small craft was crumpled under the liner's guard and for a few seconds it was feared she might be sunk.

The author was never a victim of mal de mer off Point Judith, nor ever in personal peril on the COMMONWEALTH. Nevertheless, our family can never forget one terrifying hour aboard that steamer on a calm summer night in 1935. We had taken our first-born, three-year-old David, out of New York on the COMMONWEALTH for a week end in Boston. Returning, the author, as usual, stationed himself on the forward dome deck immediately below the pilothouse, acting the role of captain leaving Fall River. The tiny lad soon became bored and was greatly frightened at the blasts of the deep-throated whistle. He insisted upon leaving, and his mother departed with him for a tour of the ship. In about fifteen minutes, anguish in her voice, she rushed back to my breezy place of vigil, reporting that David had run ahead of her in one of the lengthy corridors and could not be located. She had called his name, searched diligently on all decks, and had inquired of passengers and stewards if they had seen an adventurous curly-haired boy on the loose. Naturally, I was deeply concerned, but felt sure that he could not have fallen overboard because it was still daylight, there were many passengers on deck, and someone would have given the alarm. However, there was the frightening possibility that, searching for the engine room, he had fallen down some companionway or been unknowingly locked in a stateroom. I began a quick tour of the ship while Mrs. McAdam went searching in the opposite direction.

My first stop was the engine room because on the eastbound voyage Chief Engineer McQueen had taken us on a personally conducted tour. David had been fascinated by the massive, moving machinery. Learning that he had not been seen there I hastened up three stairways to the after upper deck. I began peering in all the dining room windows, doubtless looking like some hungry beggar hoping for crumbs. No familiar blond curly head was revealed by my snooping.

The steamer was then nearing Newport and I was about to go to the Purser's Office, requesting that someone be stationed at every gangway to make certain the child did not wander ashore while docked there.

A passenger, sitting in the Adams Salon, at the foot of the dining room stairway, noticed my perturbation, and inquired, "Are you looking for a lost boy? I saw one go up these stairs quite awhile ago." I ascended to the dining room, to be met by gracious Head Waiter Haskins. No unaccompanied little boy was anywhere about, he said. Rather insistently I asked if I might make a detailed search. Haskins stepped to the door of the adjoining grill room, where the Wharton-Ford dance orchestra was holding forth. After a quick glance he turned and inquired, "Is that your boy over there?" He pointed to a youngster sitting alongside of, but largely hidden by, the cellist. It was our "lost" David having the time of his young life! Promising him that we would return to the enchanted spot after we found "Mommy," we went in search of his frantic mother. Soon there was a happy reunion and a return to the alluring grill room.

There it developed that the tiny boy, bursting in out of nowhere had received a warm reception when he suddenly sat down next to the cellist. The musician had a son of his own about the same age as David, and between renditions he listened eagerly to David's chatter about his playmates and other childhood affairs of state. The bartender made a party out of it by indulging the happy lad with luscious maraschino cherries. Because he was perfectly safe and having such a joyful visit with his new-found friends, our young David simply could not understand why anybody thought he was "lost."

Contrasting types of Sound steamers at New York piers. Single-screw New Hampshire and big sidewheeler Providence, left. Starin Line (N. Y.-New Haven) freighter Yale, right

Popular John F. Ward, first Purser

Stanis Hoppé, long the orchestra leader

Chief Engineer John McQueen

Purser E. J. Flynn also made final voyage on Colonial's ARROW

FAMOUS COMMONWEALTH PERSONALITIES

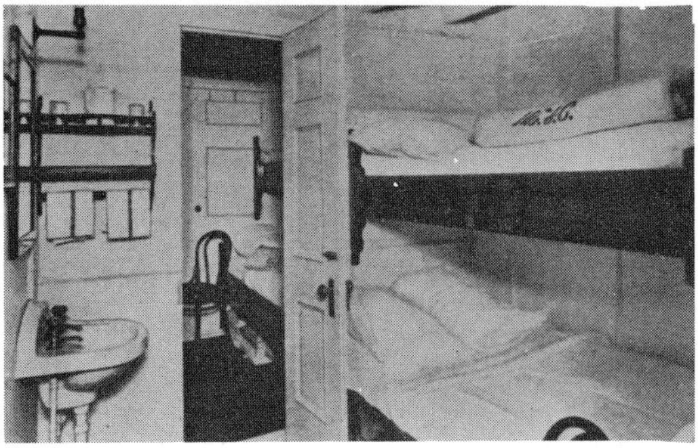

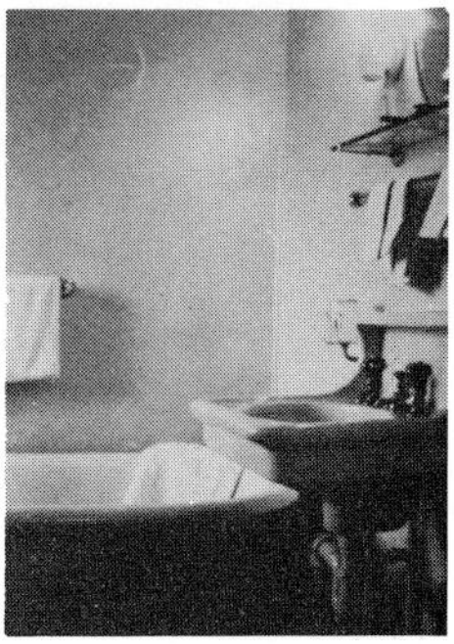

In 1927 all Fall River staterooms, regular (left) or parlor, had hot and cold running water

Dance floors came to staid Fall River Line, 1932. PLYMOUTH's shown

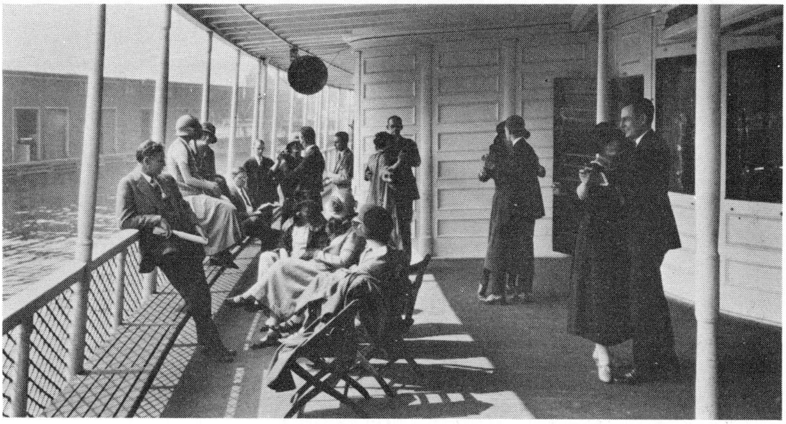

An "innovation" on the PRISCILLA—music amplified to all salons and decks

Eastern's crowded NEW YORK leaves India Wharf, Boston

THOUSAND SAILED THE SOUND NIGHTLY

Fall River's spacious PRISCILLA takes hundreds from New York

Colonial's COMET on a "sold-out" night at Providence

COMMONWEALTH'S 12,000 horsepower double-inclined compound engine. Left: Extraordinary shot of massive machinery from fifty feet above

Unusual COMMONWEALTH views. Pilot-house showing binnacle and steam-steering gear forward

Capacious freight deck (633 tons)—equivalent to train of sixty-three cars

Her crowning achievement! Broad windows show "roof top" Dining Room location

Outside staterooms, gallery deck

SUSPENSION

FALL RIVER LINE

Including

RAIL AND MOTOR COACH CONNECTIONS

EFFECTIVE JULY 20, 1937

(All Times Shown Eastern Standard)

Account of labor trouble Fall River Line Steamer Service between New York and Newport, R. I. and Fall River, Mass. is temporarily suspended.

Fall River Line Cape Special leaving Taunton at 6:42 A. M. daily for Middleboro and Hyannis and leaving Hyannis at 4:00 P. M. daily for Middleboro and Taunton is annulled between Taunton and Hyannis.

Fall River Line Special (Boston) leaving Fall River Wharf at 6:10 A. M. daily and leaving Boston at 5:00 P. M. daily is annulled between Fall River and Fall River Wharf.

Train leaving Fall River Wharf at 5:10 A. M. Saturdays only for New Bedford Wharf and train leaving New Bedford Wharf at 6:00 P. M. daily for Fall River Wharf are annulled.

N. E. T. Co. bus leaving Fall River Wharf at 5:20 A. M. except Saturdays for New Bedford Wharf and bus leaving Fall River Wharf at 7:00 A. M. daily for New Bedford Wharf are annulled.

N. E. T. Co. busses leaving Fall River Wharf at 5:55 A. M. and 6:55 A. M. for Providence, and leaving Providence at 6:23 P. M. and 6:55 P. M. for Fall River Wharf, will continue between Providence Terminal and Fall River Terminal as regular operations of the New England Transportation Company.

N. E. T. Co. bus leaving Hyannis at 8:05 A. M. and Yarmouth at 8:20 A. M. for Provincetown will leave Hyannis at 6:30 A. M. and Yarmouth at 6:42 A. M. on Tuesdays, Thursdays, and Saturdays connecting with NIGHT CAPE CODDER from New York previous night.

N. E. T. Co. bus leaving Provincetown at 2:20 P. M. daily for Yarmouth and Hyannis will leave at 7:05 P. M. and run on Tuesdays and Thursdays only connecting with NIGHT CAPE CODDER. On Sundays connection for NIGHT CAPE CODDER from Provincetown will be by train leaving at 6:40 P. M. as at present.

See New Haven R. R. timetables for through rail service between New York and Cape Cod Points with steamer connections to and from islands of Martha's Vineyard and Nantucket.

The NEW HAVEN R. R.

The NEW ENGLAND STEAMSHIP COMPANY

TO BE POSTED UNTIL AUGUST 20, 1937

The "unbelievable" poster! "Sit-down" strikes brought suspension, then abandonment of ninety-year service

Going, going, gone! COMMONWEALTH's costly furnishings were auctioned. Left: Grand Salon. Right: Louis XV Salon stripped bare

"For whom the bell tolls"

Inert giantess dragged from Fall River, Jan. 1938

Fall River Wharf, silent and deserted, was once a gateway for all New England

Forever enshrined! Flagship's stern carvings at The Mariners' Museum, Virginia

CHAPTER TWELVE

Peril off Point Judith

October 1925 was a rather bad month for the COMMONWEALTH. Twice within weeks the paddlewheel on her port side unexpectedly misbehaved, requiring the steamer to be anchored and put under the leash of tugs. The second mechanical failure, occurring while the COMMONWEALTH was fighting her way to New York in a furious southwesterly gale, was fraught with real danger.

On the morning of October 9, within minutes of completing her voyage to Pier 14, North River, trouble developed in the port wheel as the COMMONWEALTH was passing under Brooklyn Bridge. Captain Robinson anchored near the Battery and sent for tugs to tow the liner to the Fulton Street terminal.

Norman L. Strickland, youngest of COMMONWEALTH's regular masters, sailed approximately 15,000 nights on Long Island Sound passenger and freight steamers. Ask him to tell you of his most thrilling experience and his reply is instantaneous—"The wild night when the COMMONWEALTH was helpless in a raging sea."

Eastbound early Sunday morning, October 25, the COMMONWEALTH had been tossed about by a lashing southeast storm, the worst type in the Point Judith-Newport sector. All day Sunday the storm, called an "old grayback" by mariners, raged off the New England coast. That night the COMMONWEALTH sailed on time from Fall River and met choppy seas in the sheltered waters en route to Newport. When she arrived at Long Wharf, a troublesome spot in a high wind, the wind suddenly shifted to west and increased in velocity. At that season of the year, Sunday night westbound usually meant a "sold out" steamer. Scores of passengers boarded the liner at Newport, adding to the hundreds already aboard. Captain Robinson, who had faced worse nights leaving Newport, felt he was taking no extraordinary risk in putting out into the ocean. However, it was destined to be a night that Captain "Bob," his officers and the hundreds of passengers would always remember. For them the Psalmist's words became very real:

> "They that go down to the sea in ships . . .
> These see the works of the Lord, and
> his wonders in the deep. For at his word
> the stormy wind ariseth, which lifteth
> up the waves thereof. They are carried
> up to the heaven, and down again to the
> deep . . ."

It was a cruel sea the COMMONWEALTH met off Beaver Tail Lighthouse. Passengers walking in the wide, richly carpeted corridors, now filled with the sound of creaks and groans, were hurled to and fro. Those regaling themselves in the high dining and grill rooms warily watched as waiters approached with laden trays, and were never quite sure where their next mouthful was going.

At the blinking and moaning Point Judith Whistling Buoy the wind became a hellish cry of fury, whipping up tremendous seas and sending spray slapping up against the COMMONWEALTH's lofty pilothouse windows. The big craft rolled heavily, at times imposing a terrific strain on the engine by lifting one wheel entirely out of the sea. Shortly after the madly bobbing whistling buoy was left astern, there was a sharp, reverberating report, followed by a fearful banging in the port wheel box. The experienced ears of veteran Chief Engineer Sheldon sensed at once that the wheel had been mangled by the angry seas. He immediately stopped the powerful machinery as the worried voice of First Pilot Junior Grade Thomas Nelson, on watch, came through the speaking tube. Glumly Nelson turned to Captain "Bob," telling him that Sheldon's report was very bad. Sheldon was unable to say whether the heavy steel buckets had been smashed by ponderous waves, by submerged wreckage picked up by the revolving wheel, or if the damage was an aftermath of the breakdown in the East River shortly before. But the effect was a thousand times more important than the cause. The engine was plainly out of commission under terrifying circumstances.

Neither the pilothouse nor the engine room had any illusions as to the peril they faced. They were in a bad spot, but the passengers must not be given that impression. With characteristic coolness, which soon had a reassuring effect on the frightened travelers, Captain Robinson gave decisive orders to the superior officers in all departments. First Mate William J. Ronan was commanded to "let go both anchors," close all portholes and secure every movable object on the freight deck. The wireless operator was ordered to send out an immediate S O S. Pilot Nelson was instructed to call First Pilot Senior Grade Strickland and the entire crew to stand by for emergency duty. Patrols were doubled to guard against the possibility of fires. Chief Steward John J. O'Connell was told to extinguish the kitchen ranges and that passengers must be cautioned against smoking, since the roaring gale could make cigarette sparks very dangerous. The voyagers, many of them now seasick, were to be informed that the COMMONWEALTH was in no danger, and that, while they faced some hours of discomfort, aid was on the way. By radio, word went to Newport Repair Shops that the steamer would have to be towed to Long Wharf and that they should be prepared to make major repairs to the wheel. A special New Haven train was assembled there to take the passengers to New York.

While the COMMONWEALTH pitched, frequently dipping her bow under the huge waves, Captain Robinson was greatly relieved to know that his helpless ship was not dragging her anchors. These seasoned mariners are unbelievably taciturn! That night the COMMONWEALTH was exposed to the savagery of nature as never before. She heaved, plunged, and shook, often taking a solid wall of crashing water aboard. But Captain Strickland, admitting it was the worst night of his experience, dismisses the 1925 peril in Block Island Sound with the terse comment, "The sea was damn high with plenty of spray. The COMMONWEALTH was a real good sea boat and rode very nicely."

Few passengers that eerie autumn night felt that "she rode very nicely." They were scared. Most of them wondered if their life insurance premiums were paid up to date. How much more merciless pounding could the COMMONWEALTH take? The groaning of her frames and joiner work, sweet music to the mariners, was dirgelike to the terrified landlubbers.

The late Theodore E. Steinway, of the celebrated piano firm, a westbound voyager almost every Sunday night, while confident that the COMMONWEALTH would not founder, especially recalled the weird noises as the steamer reeled. "How those forty thousand window sash weights went 'clunkety-clunk' all night long! The real Fall River ship to ride a storm was the PLYMOUTH.[1]"

Shortly before dawn the eastbound PRISCILLA, running late in the heavy going, passed her helpless companion. She made no attempt to stop because Captain Robinson had wirelessed Captain Fred M. Hamlen that the COMMONWEALTH was in no immediate danger and there was no need for the PRISCILLA even to stand by. At about 9:30 A.M. the Coast Guard cutter MOJAVE and the Merritt-Chapman & Scott Corporation's powerful tug COMMISSIONER arrived. Coast Guard cutters ACUSHNET and RED WING also responded. The MOJAVE, the tug COMMISSIONER, and a smaller tug from Newport took the bucking COMMONWEALTH in tow. The COMMONWEALTH was dipping so deeply that, at times, only her tall smokestacks[2] were visible to the approaching rescue vessels.

[1] Captain Strickland thought the COMMONWEALTH the best sea boat, although the PLYMOUTH enjoyed that reputation.

[2] Tops of stacks were eighty-two feet above the water.

The slow trip back into Newport, while rough, was uneventful. Several hundred relieved passengers crossed the gang plank at Long Wharf. They had seen the Atlantic Ocean and Block Island Sound cause the big COMMONWEALTH to rise to the heavens, slide down into the depths, all the while diving and twisting. One of the fearful passengers said, "It was a trip through hell!" Theodore Steinway and Sidney Mitchell, president of the United Paperboard Company, acting as spokesmen, were "unstinting in praise for the fine seamanship and calm courage of Captain Robinson." Commendation for Captain "Bob" came from J. Howland Gardner, who once again knew that his COMMONWEALTH was a real ship.

Except for the smashed paddlewheel, which had abruptly changed a rough trip into a highly perilous one, the COMMONWEALTH sustained practically no damage from her hours of pounding. The PROVIDENCE and the PLYMOUTH were at Newport Shops being overhauled for winter service. Consequently, the twin-screw CITY OF LOWELL was pressed into service for a few trips. It is said that several regular Fall River Line patrons, holding stateroom tickets for the COMMONWEALTH, sniffed in disdain at the substitution of the LOWELL and flounced off Pier 14, hieing themselves to Grand Central Terminal to board a train.

Soon the COMMONWEALTH was back in service, but she seemed hoodooed. Making her last eastbound trip of the season, January 4, 1926, the COMMONWEALTH was in collision beyond Hell Gate with a New Haven Railroad tug which was shepherding two unwieldy carfloats. When the steamer was ready to leave Pier 14, visibility was not too good. However, Captain Robinson and First Pilot Senior Grade Strickland "could see Jersey"[3] and the COMMONWEALTH cast off for her regular voyage and subsequent winter hibernation at Newport Shops. Off the Brooklyn Navy Yard a thick fog covered the

[3] If any Jersey City lights could be seen it was felt safe to leave Pier 14 in fog.

East River, but the COMMONWEALTH passed successfully through tricky Hell Gate. Between Sunken Meadows and North Brother Island the COMMONWEALTH was stopped and drifting when suddenly the balky carfloats loomed up. After the impact the COMMONWEALTH, her bow somewhat twisted, anchored until the fog lifted, when she returned to Pier 14. Transferring perishable freight and her two hundred passengers to the RICHARD PECK, the COMMONWEALTH went to the dry dock next morning. At the same time, as scheduled, the PROVIDENCE went on the line at Fall River.

The COMMONWEALTH and the smaller PLYMOUTH played tit for tat in the next few months. During the height of the summer season (August 2, 1926) COMMONWEALTH broke a shaft and was relieved by the PLYMOUTH. The following December, the PLYMOUTH broke down[4] and the COMMONWEALTH became a winter boat for several weeks.

As told, the COMMONWEALTH had been in dire peril during a storm off the Rhode Island coast in October 1925. Three years later she was in jeopardy in the supposedly harmless waters of Newport harbor. A fierce southwest gale blew up on the morning of January 25, 1928. About 3 A.M. Albert Haas, then assistant superintendent of the Newport Repair Shops, received the incredible telephone message that the COMMONWEALTH had broken loose and was headed for the mud flats and rocks off the city's Elm Street Pier. Haas drove rapidly to the COMMONWEALTH's winter berth (Briggs Wharf) to find the stern of the liner more than a hundred feet away from the wharf. Miraculously her bow hawsers were holding against the pressure of the howling gale. To Haas's amazement he found that the venturesome COMMONWEALTH had torn away a forty-ton granite mooring and pulled out mooring piles like teeth. An engineering crew of about a dozen men was on the steamer but was able to do little to impede her most unexpected

[4] After 1906 fire, PLYMOUTH, rebuilt on original hull, had considerable mechanical difficulty.

voyage. About twenty shop employees, who had rushed to the scene, attempted with their puny but united strength to pull the stern back into position until tugs could be summoned. It was probably the most uneven tug of war Rhode Island had ever seen! Daylight found three tugs pulling with every ounce of power to hold the big ship from beaching. Finally someone suggested that stout hawsers be carried some two hundred fifty feet to the big engine of the shop's giant crane, a Newport landmark. With this mighty power from the shore and the tugs fighting into the head wind, the COMMONWEALTH was slowly swung off the flats and pulled inch by inch back to her berth. By noon the "runaway" was snugged down with new hawsers. For hours the task of saving the COMMONWEALTH seemed utterly impossible.

Captain Strickland, then first pilot senior grade on the PLYMOUTH, vividly remembers the appalling sight of a handful of men attempting to hold the wandering six thousand-ton steamer against an almost irresistible gale. He described the storm as "terrible" and said the PLYMOUTH was the only east-bound steamer to come around Point Judith that morning. When Captain Robinson guided the PLYMOUTH, then over an hour late, around Newport's Torpedo Station the mariners noted immediately that the stern light of the moored COMMONWEALTH was not in its usual range. They were dumbfounded to see that the flagship, their summer assignment, was out of control and in danger of piling up on the rocky shore. But their immediate concentration had to be given to thwarting the gale by expertly maneuvering the PLYMOUTH alongside Long Wharf. That difficult task accomplished, Robinson and Strickland, from their own pilothouse, watched the heroic efforts of Haas's men with anxiety and admiration.

While reboilering at Newport Shops, April 26, 1929, the COMMONWEALTH caused a midnight alarm when fire was discovered close to a temporary stack. For a few seconds another

[5] For details of PLYMOUTH fire, March 1906, see Chapter 1.

PLYMOUTH conflagration[5] was feared. A main deck donkey boiler supplied steam for the COMMONWEALTH's fire pumps which went into immediate action. The blaze had been drowned by the ship's skeleton crew before the Newport firemen roared onto Briggs Wharf.

Captain Robinson, one of the most popular of the COMMONWEALTH's regular masters, was on sick leave during most of 1932, Norman Strickland serving in his place at the middle window. At the age of sixty-one, Robinson died in New Bedford on December 10. Born in Newburgh, on the Hudson, Captain "Bob" had sailed Long Island Sound for forty-two years. Captain Daniel Barrett, of the PRISCILLA, relieved the youthful Strickland early in 1933. Barrett had the COMMONWEALTH in the summer, the PROVIDENCE in the winter, for nearly two years. After Barrett's death in March 1935, Strickland was made the COMMONWEALTH's commander and served with distinction until a month before the Fall River Line ceased operation.

In 1937 the bankrupt New Haven Railroad applied to the Federal Court for permission to abandon all services of the subsidiary New England Steamship Company, except the Fall River Line, the New Haven Line (freight), and the Vineyard Line (New Bedford to Martha's Vineyard and Nantucket). When the Providence Line was terminated in May, Captains Frank H. Avery and Philip Ollweiler, senior mariners of the company, became commanders of the COMMONWEALTH and PRISCILLA respectively. Despite their seniority, these skippers had preferred the New York-Providence run, presumably to avoid directing the every-other-morning's 3 A.M. docking at difficult Long Wharf, Newport.

Little did they, or anyone else, realize they had only a few weeks to serve!

C H A P T E R T H I R T E E N

An Era Closes

Methodist Bishop John Wesley Lord, of Boston, then gracing a New Jersey pulpit, once reviewed the author's *The Old Fall River Line* before a literary society. The cleric was one of those unfortunates who had never traveled on the Fall River Line. He concluded his discussion with the ringing words, "After reading this book I wonder why the Fall River Line was ever allowed to die." Doubtless hundreds of thousands of Fall River Line patrons have asked themselves the same question.

To the week-after-week, year-after-year, regular travelers on the steamers, the abrupt and unbelievable termination of the Fall River Line remains a sore point to this day. A decade after the COMMONWEALTH and the PRISCILLA had unceremoniously gone to the boneyard, the "regulars" could hardly accept the fact. The ten-year lapse had not softened the blow for two former Fall River adherents, one adjacent to New York's Hell Gate, the other residing in the far-off San Francisco. By sheer coincidence these men, three thousand miles apart, presumably unknown to each other, wrote the author in 1947 expressing their personal conviction in almost identical words. In a letter from New York's Theodore E. Steinway was this sentiment: "*With the passing of the Fall River Line something fine and gracious has gone out of our lives.*" A few days later, Paul L. Henchey, a transplanted New Englander, wrote from San Francisco, "*Something fine and beautiful went out of life with the passing of the Fall River Line.*" Two hearts reacting as one!

In the face of testimony of this kind, why was the Fall River Line allowed to die? It must be remembered that for almost the last half of its long career the Fall River Line was owned by a monopolistic railroad which ultimately got into financial difficulty. The Old Colony, owner of the steamers after the Jim Fisk era, a railroad which "dwelt sweetly in the memories of all New Englanders,"[1] was never the same after the New Haven leased it. The Gardners, Nickersons, Walls, and Haas's had to accept policy set by railroad men. It is common knowledge that many high New Haven officials were indifferent, if not downright antagonistic, to the subsidiary steamer lines.

The merry, madcap Morgan-Mellen days, out of which COMMONWEALTH was born (336 New Haven subsidiary corporations, remember) brought inevitable bankruptcy in 1935. In 1937 the Interstate Commerce Commission, reviewing the cause of the New Haven's debacle, went straight back to its 1913 investigation. It said:

> "We predicted that, in addition to substantial losses already incurred, the property of the New Haven would be called upon *for many years to make up the drain upon its resources* resulting from financial transactions outside the field in which stockholders supposed their moneys were invested. That this prediction was based on a sound premise has been demonstrated clearly by the record in this (1937) investigation." [Author's italics]

It is difficult to say who was more responsible for the trend away from all New England coastal steamers—Henry Ford or the arbiters of women's fashions. When the author first knew the Fall River Line, and continuing until after World War I, there was a New York-Fall River freight steamer in both directions six nights a week in addition to the daily freight-carrying passenger liner.[2] Cotton was an ever-present

[1] *Steelways of New England,* Alvin F. Harlow: Creative Age Press, 1946.

[2] Total capacity in each direction about two thousand tons. CITY OF TAUNTON closed freight service, February 1924.

cargo—bales from the South eastbound, print goods from Fall River and New Bedford westbound. When fashionable women forsook cotton as dress material, and high labor costs became the rule, the textile industry faded away from southern New England. By 1922 New Haven's President E. J. Pearson was complaining of the competition of the private automobile and motor trucks during favorable weather.

When fast train service was inaugurated along the Connecticut shore in 1852 a pompous spellbinder in New London trumpeted, "Fellow citizens, ought we not to rejoice that we are now within two hours of New Haven? Young America, are you contented or is this not fast enough for you?" The twenty-knot "nautical royalty of 1907"—BUNKER HILL, COMMONWEALTH, HARVARD, MASSACHUSETTS and YALE—gave almost "express-train speed afloat." The opening of the Cape Cod Canal in 1916 reduced the time of the Boston-New York overnight voyage to thirteen and one-half hours. But by 1920 neither young America nor their elders were "contented" with any such sluggishness. Thirteen and one half hours was definitely "not fast enough."

As automobile motors and tires improved, servicing became more plentiful and highways more durable; leisurely modes of travel, even in the grand manner, became less appealing. The families of two of my prep school[3] classmates, Willan C. Roux and Frederick S. Osborne, for years had traveled by steamer, New York to Fall River, thence by train to destination. The Rouxs spent their summers in Maine; the Osbornes, under the shadow of famous Highland Light, Cape Cod. The author well remembers Fred Osborne's "daring" announcement that the Osbornes were driving from Newark through to North Truro and *hoped to make it in one day!* They did not love the Fall River Line any less but . . .

That the Rouxs and the Osbornes were multiplied a thousandfold is demonstrated by an inspection of the passenger

[3] Newark (N. J.) Academy, Class of 1919.

traffic figures of the Eastern's Boston Line, the Colonial Line, and the Fall River Line. Fall River's peak year was 1906, when three other steamer lines sailed nightly between New York and Fall River and travel on "America's most famous inland water route" was at bargain rates. That year, 444,500 passengers were transported by the Fall River Line. In the COMMONWEALTH's first full season of operation (1909), despite the severe competition of the HARVARD and YALE on the "outside line," Fall River's total for the year just missed 400,000. In 1920, the second summer of Fall River "double service" (four passenger ships in operation), one more good night (667 passengers) would have added up to 400,000 Fall River Line voyagers. Except for the war year, 1918, when schedules were disrupted by Navy port regulations at Newport, and timid travelers feared attacks by German U-boats, the Fall River steamers carried over 300,000 annually from 1900 to 1924. (Incidentally, 1918 was the summer the Metropolitan Line ceased advertising that it was the "outside line to Boston"; then its copy stressed "always in sight of land.") The advent of the new steamers NEW YORK and BOSTON on the direct run between those cities in 1924 dropped the Fall River total to 299,774; it never exceeded 300,000 again. In 1936, the last full year of operation, the Fall River Line collected tickets from only 127,794 passengers. However, in all fairness it must be pointed out that unusually severe ice conditions brought an unprecedented suspension of Fall River Line passenger service for about three weeks, reducing the passenger traffic by several thousand.

With the coming of the 1929 depression, J. Howland Gardner's world was smashed into as many pieces as had his wife's birthday present some years before. That tale, never alluded to in the presence of Gardner, was a New England Steamship Company classic. Gardner went to Tiffany's to purchase an expensive clock as a gift for his wife. He was enamored of three but could not be certain which would have the greatest appeal to Mrs. Gardner. Consequently, the steamship executive paid for one clock and took two on approval. He hurried to

Grand Central Terminal, arranged with a New Haven official to have a Shore Line express stopped at Lyme, Connecticut, gave the bulky package to the Pullman porter with the explicit instructions that the train would stop at Lyme and the station agent would be waiting to receive the valuable parcel. Every phase of the arrangements was thoroughly "protected." However, something went wrong and the train sped through Lyme at sixty miles an hour. The puzzled porter followed instructions; the package was to be put off at Lyme. He flung the box toward the astonished station agent, who proved to be no Joe DiMaggio in a spectacular attempt at a shoestring catch. In a second, springs, hands, and minute parts of the clocks covered the Lyme platform. It was Mrs. Gardner's most expensive gift—J. Howland Gardner had to pay for three clocks that never ticked in his home!

Yes, J. Howland Gardner's world was cracking up. His whole life had been lived in the atmosphere of the world-famous Sound steamers. His father, a deep-sea captain, had later become general superintendent of the combined Sound fleet. The son, a native of Newport, had been successively assistant to George Peirce, designer of five Fall River passenger steamers,[4] superintendent of marine construction at Newport, operating vice president at Pier 14, New York, and president of the New England Steamship Company.

The pronounced trend away from the Sound steamers, especially in the winter months, was accelerated by the depression of 1929. In 1926, the New England Steamship Company had shown a small deficit of $29,688.33. The figures were in the black by about $50,000 at the close of the next year. From that point on, the railroad accountants in New Haven posted the steamer line's annual reports in the color of blood. In February 1931, Gardner retired as president of the New England Steamship Company, after thirty-seven years of association with the

[4] Peirce designed PILGRIM, PURITAN, PLYMOUTH, PRISCILLA, PROVIDENCE; several freighters.

Fall River Line. His place at Pier 14 was taken by John H. Lofland, with the title, General Manager. In his final message to the steamship employees Gardner wrote in part:

> "We have a wonderful organization. It has always stood for safe and dependable transportation. During my many years of service, I am proud to say I have never found it necessary to go outside this company to hire anyone to take the place of a licensed officer. As evidence of the high standing and efficiency of our licensed officers, it has been found necessary to discharge only three during my entire administration. . . . I want you who are in command of steamers, as well as the younger officers who must take your places, to remember the past record and to hold that record as a heritage."

Gardner might be criticized for one characteristic, ultra-conservatism. At the risk of touching off a controversy, this author expresses the conviction that the Fall River Line could have held its own against the Eastern Steamship Lines competition, had an immediate modernization program for the Fall River Line steamers been instituted in 1924. For example, Gardner stoutly opposed conversion of the Fall River sidewheelers to oil fuel, claiming an increase in the fire hazard or panic resulting from flashbacks and heavy smoke. The author well recalls being in the vice president's office, Pier 14, the noon the MORRO CASTLE burned off New Jersey. First news reports, just trickling in, blamed the conflagration on lightning striking the liner's fuel tanks. J. Everett Benson, one of the Fall River Line's best technical men, and John Zeto spoke of Gardner's firm conviction that oil and passenger steamers did not mix. Consequently, the big sidewheeler continued to burn some sixty tons of coal nightly, necessitating engine room forces of over forty men, not to mention showering the upper decks with cinders.

When the magnificent new steamers NEW YORK and Bos-

TON came to the Eastern's direct Boston run in 1924, they had hot and cold running water in their many deluxe staterooms and cold running water in all others. (The smaller Colonial Line steamers CONCORD and LEXINGTON had pioneered with cold running water in all rooms in 1910.) For all its vaunted luxury, Fall River Line travelers had to depend on pitchers of water for their ablutions, and the men had to ring for hot water for shaving.

Before Charles W. Morse had sent his HARVARD and YALE racing around Cape Cod, the Fall River Line had suffered no particular geographical disadvantage. Prior to the Joy Line's short-lived direct service with the plodding OLD DOMINION and the advent of Morse's flyers in 1907, all steamer passengers arriving in Boston came part way by train, arriving from Norwich, Stonington, Providence, or Fall River. Arising at ungodly hours to take trains from the ports was an accepted nuisance. But Eastern's new steamers in 1924 afforded two or three hours more sleep eastbound, modern travel luxury, and dancing. The new generation made the Eastern first choice.

The New Haven Railroad-New England Steamship Company 1924-25 attitude seemed to be that when the "fad" of riding on the NEW YORK and BOSTON wore off, passengers would return in droves to the superior service of the Fall River Line. It just did not work out that way. Slow to act, the Fall River Line went all the way when it did! Hot and cold running water in every stateroom on every Fall River Line steamer was installed at Newport in the winter of 1926,[5] spring of 1927. This major operation reputedly cost a half-million dollars. The Fall River Line became the only service with both hot and cold running water in every stateroom.

The new 1924 Eastern steamers had upper deck ballrooms and featured dancing as an evening diversion. The "jazz age" had come, but the Gardner regime refused to recognize it.

[5] PLYMOUTH installation, December 17, 1926; PROVIDENCE, January 25, 1927.

Dancing was taboo on the Fall River Line until 1932! The younger generation found the Fall River Line prim and staid. The author recalls the near bitterness with which R. Harry Pusch, general passenger agent, called for jazz and not "dirges" by the Fall River Line orchestras. From 1924 until 1932 the Fall River Line resisted any "night club atmosphere." Then dance floors were installed on the gallery decks of the PROVIDENCE and PLYMOUTH, in the grill room of the COMMONWEALTH, and the dining room of the PRISCILLA. When Lofland took the reigns he made the COMMONWEALTH the "dancingest" steamer on the Sound by installing a second dance floor. The COMMONWEALTH's main deck library was converted into an attractive Parisian sidewalk café; her grill room, three decks above, was advertised as the "roof garden." At a cost of several thousand dollars, vigorously protested by rail officials in New Haven, so it is said, Lofland had the steamers' furnishings, especially on the PRISCILLA, completely modernized. Many believe that had the hot and cold running water, modern furniture, and dance floors been installed in 1924, the Eastern's new steamers would have made no serious inroads on the Fall River Line's New York-Boston traffic. The criticism that the New Haven Railroad "did not meet competition by using its mind," was demonstrated by its Fall River Line smugness.

Rumors concerning the future of the Fall River Line abounded early in 1937. Permission to close out the Providence Line and the New Bedford Line was granted by the Federal Court. Business interests in Fall River were informed by the trustees of the bankrupt New Haven Railroad that freight tonnage on the steamers must be increased, and pledges of cooperation were given. A more extensive fire sprinkler system placed on the PRISCILLA by government edict, following the MORRO CASTLE tragedy, allayed suspicion that she was to be retired from service.

Everything seemed set for a prosperous 1937 summer for the Fall River Line. No longer would Cape Cod and Nantucket business have to be shared with the company's New Bedford Line. Bus connections were established between Fall River Wharf and Providence to insure retention of the defunct Providence Line traffic. The International Yacht Races were scheduled off Newport late in July, and a heavy advance sale was reported. An old-time "sold out most every night" summer would scotch all this idle chatter about the New Haven Railroad abandoning the Fall River Line!

A threat against continuance of the steamers came from an entirely unexpected source. The American Federation of Labor and the new CIO, led by forceful Joseph Curran, began a bitter contest for control of New York's waterfront. Passenger service on the Eastern's Boston Line was suspended for several trips, due to conflicting demands of the rival unions. Then labor unrest on the Fall River Line flared into the open. On the evening of June 30 the COMMONWEALTH had taken aboard at New York her largest passenger list of the season. The porters sang "Happy days are here again"—the steamer had over nine hundred aboard, many of whom were children en route to summer camps. Captain Frank Avery was about to give the command "Cast off," when word came that a sit-down strike by essential members of the crew had begun.[6] The westbound PRISCILLA was delayed at Fall River by the same unheard-of tactics. At Pier 14, argument and persuasion failed; the crew would not sail. They wanted more money and better living quarters. Agitated New Haven officials arranged for special trains to transport the COMMONWEALTH's perplexed passengers to New England.

The railroad trustees declared at once that any further labor difficulty would mean abandonment of the historic service. "Pure bluff," snorted the labor leaders, to be echoed by the crews who witnessed the increased traffic and heard about the lucrative Yacht Race bookings.

[6] *The Old Fall River Line*, op. cit., p. 210.

But the trustees were not fooling! On July 12 crews on the railroad's New Bedford, Martha's Vineyard, and Nantucket Line "sat down." When, in sympathy with their island steamer brethren, the crews[7] of the COMMONWEALTH at Fall River and the PRISCILLA at New York "sat down" they crushed the life out of the ninety-year-old Fall River Line.

The inactive crews refused to leave the steamers at either terminal. Strickland and other officers stood their regular watches on the idle COMMONWEALTH at Fall River. The tedium lasted for several days. Then came the "complete and awful surprise." The railroad trustees decreed suspension of the service and the paying off of the crews. The COMMONWEALTH never moved again under her own power!

As the veterans of the service reluctantly trudged off the COMMONWEALTH, it all seemed a preposterous hoax, an effort by the company to bring the strikers to their knees. But in a few days public officials and civic leaders in Fall River, Newport, and New Bedford were appalled when the trustees sought Federal Court ratification of their determination to abandon the service. There was to be no compromise, no negotiation, no resumption on any basis. On July 27, Federal Judge Carroll C. Hincks, sitting in New Haven, heard the trustee's "prayer for relief." The jurist also heard, but was unmoved by, eloquent pleas for resumption of the service by George L. Sisson, Corporation Counsel of Fall River, and Jeremiah A. Sullivan, Newport City Solicitor. Judge Hincks granted the petition and authorized the trustees to dispose of the six passenger steamers and the three freighters comprising the New England Steamship Company's Sound fleet.

The next morning in the long Grand Central Terminal corridor, Charles F. Clark, New Haven passenger official, almost had a head-on collision with a white-mustached man abruptly leaving the private office of R. Harry Pusch. Before coming to

[7] Licensed officers did not participate in the strike.

head the parent railroad's passenger organization, Pusch for years had been the popular general passenger agent of the Fall River Line at Pier 14. "Ye gods, what did Harry do to that man!," mused Clark, noticing that the dazed stranger was sad of countenance. Clark's curiosity was short-lived, because Pusch's buzzer rang for him.

"Did you just see a man leaving my office?" inquired Pusch.

"I sure did; gee, you must have given him a rough time. It almost looked to me as if he was crying."

"Well, damn it all, he was crying—in case you don't know it that was my old boss, J. Howland Gardner. He's all broken up about the terrible end of the Fall River Line. And I feel like hell about it myself! We were having a regular wake in here; J. H. was blubbering all over the place. Neither of us thought we'd outlive the Fall River Line!"

Why shouldn't the resolute Gardner give way to grief? He and the COMMONWEALTH had been an almost inseparable pair. Three decades before Judge Hincks' fateful decision and his emotional commiseration with Harry Pusch, Gardner had been directed by Pierpont Morgan and Charles S. Mellen to build a steamer greater than PRISCILLA, *and he had done so!*

For twenty-nine years Gardner had observed his handiwork severely tested by collisions, groundings, gales, and wild seas, but always triumphant. He had seen the COMMONWEALTH steam more than a million miles, carry some ten million persons without loss of a single one, invariably arriving on time. He himself had been aboard the brand-new COMMONWEALTH when she sank the big VOLAND and gallantly rescued the foundered ship's crew. On vacation in the west in 1924, he had heard with pride how his COMMONWEALTH had virtually borne the sinking BOSTON on her back into the safety of Newport. Now the great sidewheeler, a masterpiece of shipbuilding, beloved of travelers, as staunch and seaworthy as ever, still the largest steamer in the New England service, was destined for the scrap heap!

On Saturday morning, January 8, 1938, the author's phone rang. An executive of the New York towing concern which had already lugged the PROVIDENCE and the PLYMOUTH from Newport to a wrecking yard in Baltimore said, "The COMMONWEALTH will be towed through Hell Gate at two o'clock this afternoon." The author expressed surprise that the COMMONWEALTH was being towed via Long Island Sound and the East River. He knew that two smaller sidewheelers had gone by the outside route to Baltimore. He was told that on Thursday evening (January 6) a few hours after the COMMONWEALTH had been pulled away from Fall River Wharf, a southeast storm blew up. The two tugs could not handle the big craft in the open sea off Block Island. Like the family horse which knew his way home, the COMMONWEALTH had learned that the only westbound way was via The Race, Long Island Sound, and Hell Gate. She imposed her will upon the tugs and the course was changed to Long Island Sound.

"The COMMONWEALTH's coming through Hell Gate at two. Let's go!" Everything else immediately became secondary. The author loaded his movie camera and, accompanied by his brother John, a COMMONWEALTH lover, and his six-year-old son David, drove immediately to New York City, parking near Gracie Mansion, now the home of New York's mayor. On the dot of two o'clock a tug appeared beneath Hell Gate Bridge. Two tall black stacks were instantly recognized a short distance behind. After the COMMONWEALTH was dragged slowly past the tip of Welfare (Blackwell's) Island, the car was rapidly driven downtown to another East River vantage point. Haltingly, the stripped and helpless COMMONWEALTH turned the river's bend near Williamsburg Bridge and disappeared into the winter sunset.

Young David, who had terrified his parents two years earlier by becoming "lost" on a very much alive COMMONWEALTH, turned his face upward and said, "Well, Daddy, we won't get any more lumps of sugar off her." (The dining room's individually wrapped lumps of sugar, adorned with the COM-

MONWEALTH's picture, had been prize booty for the lad on his too few exciting voyages.)

No more lumps of COMMONWEALTH sugar. What a discerning observation the child had voiced! Even in his tender years, he sensed that life had been sweetened by voyages on the COMMONWEALTH, *Giantess of Long Island Sound!*

STEAMER COMMONWEALTH

Date launched	October 9, 1907
Date commissioned	July 1, 1908
Construction material, hull	Steel
Length overall	455 ft. 8 inches
Length moulded	437 ft. 10 inches
Beam over guards	94 ft. 7 inches
Beam moulded	55 ft.
Depth	22 ft.
Mean draft, light	13 ft.
Mean draft, loaded	14 ft. 6 inches
Displacement	5,410 tons
Maximum speed (statute miles)	23 miles
General contractors	Quintard Iron Works
Builders of hull	Wm. A. Cramp & Sons
Builders of machinery	Wm. A. Cramp & Sons
Builders of wheels	Quintard Iron Works
Builders of joiner work	Pottier & Stymus
Designer	Newport Shops, Fall River Line, J. Howland Gardner, Supt. of Marine Construction
Consulting engineer	Stevenson Taylor Warren T. Berry, Supt.
Designer of interior	Pottier & Stymus
Tonnage, gross	5,980 tons
Tonnage, net	2,500 tons
Cargo, capacity in cars	63
Coal bunker capacity	200 tons

Number of life boats	12[1]
Number of life rafts	12[1]
Number of watertight bulkheads	7
Number of watertight compartments above double bottom	8
Number of watertight compartments in double bottom	46
Number of passenger staterooms	421
Number of passenger berths	1,290
Number of passengers allowed	2,000
Engines, type	Double inclined compound
Mode of propulsion	sidewheel
Cylinders, diameter	2, 50 inches 2, 96 inches
Stroke	9 ft. 6 inches
Revolutions designed	30
Indicated horsepower	12,000
Surface (two condensers)	16,060
Boilers, number of main	10[2]
Type—main boilers	S. E. Scotch
Boilers—Diameter	15 ft. 6 inches
Length	13 ft. 6 inches
Working pressure	153#
Heating surface (10 boilers)	29,340 sq. feet
Furnaces, number of	30

[1] *Number increased in 1913 to 29 life boats and 24 life rafts to provide for 1,678 persons.*

[2] *The Scotch Boilers were removed in 1929 and eight B & W watertube boilers installed.*

Furnaces, type—corrugated	54 inches diameter
Grate surface (10 boilers)	937 sq. feet
Coal consumption per hour (estimated)	8½ tons
Wheels, type	Feathering
Wheels, diameter outside buckets	31 feet
Wheels, length of buckets	14 ft. 6 inches
Wheels, width of buckets	5 feet
Number of fire bulkheads above the main deck	2, dividing vessel into 3 zones.
Sprinklers and thermostat alarms throughout the entire vessel	40 circuits

BIBLIOGRAPHY

NEWSPAPERS

BOSTON

American
Herald
News Bureau
Post

Fall River Herald News
New Haven Register
New London Day
Newport Daily News
Newport Herald
Newport Mercury
Providence Journal

NEW YORK

Herald
News
Sun
Times
Tribune
World

PERIODICALS

Colliers Weekly
Fall River Line Journal
Harpers Weekly
Marine Journal
Master, Mate and Pilot
Nautical Gazette
New York Architect (July 1908)
Seaboard Magazine
Transactions—The Society of Naval Architects and Marine Engineers
Steamboat Bill—Steamship Historical Society of America
World's Work

BOOKS AND PAMPHLETS

Allen, Frederick Lewis. *The Great Pierpont Morgan,* Harper and Brothers, 1949

Babcock, F. Lawrence. *Spanning the Atlantic,* Alfred A. Knopf, 1931

Baker, George Pierce. *The Formation of the New England Railroad Systems,* Harvard University Press, 1937

Beard, Charles A. and Mary R. *Basic History of the United States,* Blakiston Company, 1944

Brandeis, Louis D. *Financial Condition of the New York, New Haven and Hartford Railroad Company* and *The Boston and Maine Railroad,* 1907

Dayton, Fred Erving. *Steamboat Days,* Frederick A. Stokes Company, 1925

Dodman, Frank E. *Ships of the Cunard Line,* John De Graff, Inc., 1955

Eskew, Garnett Laidlaw. *Cradle of Ships,* G. P. Putnam's Sons, 1958

Fisher, Charles Eben. *Story of the Old Colony Railroad,* 1919

Gardner, J. Howland. *The Development of Steam Navigation on Long Island Sound,* 1943

Gardner, J. Howland and Berry, Warren T. *Steamer Commonwealth,* 1908

Harlow, Alvin F. *Steelways of New England,* Creative Age Press, 1946

Lief, Arthur. *Brandeis—A Personal History,* Stackpole Sons, 1936

Mason, Alpheus T. *Brandeis—A Free Man's Life,* Viking Press, 1946

Morrison, John H. *History of American Steam Navigation,* Stephen Daye Press (reprint), 1958

New York, New Haven and Hartford Railroad Company—*Annual Reports*

Satterlee, Herbert L. *J. Pierpont Morgan; An Intimate Portrait,* Macmillan, 1939

Staples, Henry Lee and Mason, Alpheus T. *The Fall of a Railroad Empire,* Syracuse University Press, 1947

Tyler, David B. *The American Clyde,* University of Delaware Press, 1958

United States—Interstate Commerce Commission
Report of Commissioner Charles A. Prouty, 1913
Report of Financial Transactions of New York, New Haven and Hartford Railroad, July 1914
Investigation of New York, New Haven and Hartford Railroad, April 1937

United States Senate—63rd Congress
Senate Document #544, February 7, 1914

Winkler, John M. *Morgan the Magnificent,* Garden City Publishing Company, 1930

INDEX

DATE DUE

CABIN PLANS — STEA

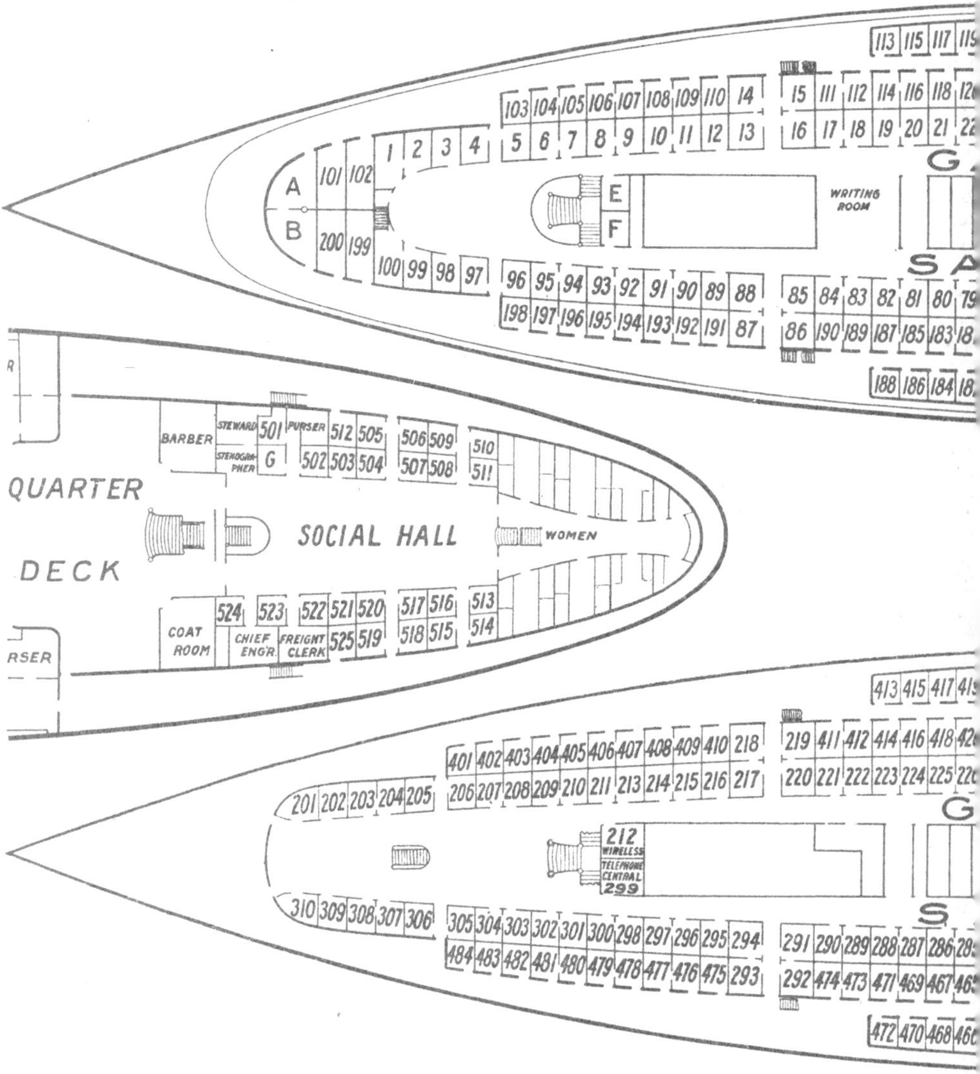